ENDORS

As a psychologist in a large private practice for over 40 years, I have found this to be a most practical book. I suggest it to most of my clients. Nearly every page contains a gem to help them get closer to their personal healing process.

— Pat Webbink, PhD,
Private Practice, Bethesda, MD

For me this book is a journey through self-exploration of the core concepts that block our living joyful, peaceful lives. It built on each idea as I read through it and was difficult to put down. The figures and tables condense the text into easy-to-understand and -interpret formats. Whether you are recovering from trauma or simply the everyday complexities of life, there is something in it for you. With all my notes and sticky tabs, I will return to this book for quite some time.

— Christy Cechman MLIS, DC, Librarian,
Centers for Disease Control
and Prevention, Atlanta, GA

Dr. Whitfield clearly and with insight describes some 15 common issues, problems or roadblocks that he has seen that cause most people's negative thinking and dysfunction. This easy-to-understand set of tools is extremely useful for therapists and self-help readers to use in their recognition and recovery work. This superb work reflects his long and valuable clinical experience.

— John Louis, Master in Counseling,
Schema Therapist, Singapore

Dr. Whitfield writes in such easy to understand language and avoids a lot of jargon. I am not a big reader of "self-help" books because I have a fear of looking inside myself, but this book made it easy to think about me and my struggles in a non-judgmental, constructive way. It has given me the courage to do some deeper thinking about myself and my life. It has given me a hope that I will not be in this dark place forever.

— Pat D., EMT (Emergency Medical
Technician) and recovering
trauma survivor

WISDOM TO KNOW THE DIFFERENCE

Core Issues in Relationships,
Recovery and Living

How to Understand Your
and Others' Common Conflicts
and
How to Heal Them

With References to Practical Psychology,
Spirituality and Twelve Step Work

Charles L. Whitfield MD

Author of
Healing the Child Within
and
***Not Crazy*: You May Not Be Mentally Ill**

𝔐ℏ𝔓
muse house press

MUSE HOUSE PRESS

ISBN: 978-1-935827-10-8

Trade Paperback (also available in Kindle)

Copyright © 2012 Charles L. Whitfield
All Rights Reserved

Visit us on the Internet at:

> www.MuseHousePress.com
> www.cbwhit.com
> www.BarbaraWhitfield.com

Muse House Press and the MHP Logo are imprints of Muse House Press.

Cover design and Interior composition by: Donald Brennan / Muse House Press / YakRider Media

Up to 5% of each chapter may be reproduced as quotes provided attribution to the author is made. Other use may be made only with prior written permission of the publisher.

Direct requests to: Muse House Press

Printed in the United States of America

Second printing

ACKNOWLEDGEMENTS

I would like to thank my patients and colleagues from whom I have learned the many dimensions about these core issues that impact us most days of our life. I hope my observations on these common roadblocks, lifetraps, concerns and problems will be useful.

DEDICATION

I dedicate this book to all people who have been in pain and have ever felt frustrated or stuck in their relationships or recovery from an addiction or any problem in living.

FOR MORE ASSISTANCE

If the going gets too rough or painful when using this book, consider finding a licensed psychotherapist or counselor to further assist you in working through your issues. If they or anyone else push you to use a psychiatric drug over identifying and working through your issues and trauma effects, consider reading about the dangers of doing so in psychiatrist Peter Breggin's or my book. [9, 103] If they do not address these areas, consider getting a second opinion.

ON THE COVER

We have lauded Wisdom through the ages as a precious human quality. We gave it a name, a gender and other human traits. Philosophers, poets, artists and leaders have in words, songs and art, elevated it to the highest status for millennia.

We have given Wisdom a special place among the languages of cultures around the world. Some of the more recognizable, descriptive terms of it are: Ἁγία Σοφία, "Holy Wisdom" in Modern Greek; Latin: *Sancta Sophia* "Sacred Wisdom," *Sancta Sapientia*; and in the Turkish: *Ayasofya* —a sacred aspiration.

We can read *about* Wisdom. We can also *see* and *hear* others *acting* with Wisdom, but we can only gain Wisdom for ourself through our own experience and firsthand knowledge.   Indeed, Wisdom comes at a high cost —we must seek it and experience it for ourselves.

On the cover, we show intersecting transparent planes and certain opposing descriptive terms in multiple dimensions. These represent the dynamic planes of life and opportunities to learn more about ourself, others and a Higher Power of our choosing. Here we show Wisdom as emanating from the bright core of our own being.

In this powerful book, Dr. Whitfield offers a practical path that can help us to experience and apprehend Wisdom for ourselves and to begin living our life more wisely and skillfully with understanding, acceptance, courage and serenity.

—dlb

TABLE OF CONTENTS

TABLE OF FIGURES

TABLE OF TABLES

TABLE OF SECTIONS

1 INTRODUCTION TO CORE ISSUES

I was inspired for this book's title by the following words:

> *God grant me the serenity*
> *To accept the things I cannot change;*
> *Courage to change the things I can;*
> *And wisdom to know the difference.*

This stanza is from Reinhold Niebuhr's classic poem, later titled *The Serenity Prayer,* and to which I will refer throughout this book.

People have defined wisdom as:

1) making the best use of our available knowledge,

2) the ability from our experience, insight and reflection to know truth and use good judgment, and

3) a well-developed form of common sense. Most psychologists regard wisdom as being different from our ordinary mental and thinking abilities. Some believe that it cannot be taught.

But I believe that wisdom can be *learned*, and in that sense that it *can* be taught. But it is mostly *self-taught*. In this book I will describe the many aspects of wisdom in recognizing, accurately naming, and working through each core issue. Here's what I have seen.

When a child grows up in a crazy (abusive, traumatic, or neglectful) family and a crazy world, several crucial things happen. Their associated emotional pain becomes so intense that the child's Real Self goes into hiding (Figure 1.1). To survive, it over-develops a false self (ego), and as part of the process it learns to use several mechanisms and dynamics to defend itself from the inordinate emotional pain that it experiences repeatedly. We can summarize and describe a large part of these defense mechanisms most simply as involving and often being core recovery issues.[1]

HEALING AND RECOVERY PRINCIPLES

The focus of healing is on several tasks, which I described in my book *Healing the Child Within* 25 years ago. (When I wrote it I knew how important core issues were, and since then I have increasingly come to appreciate the

---

[1] Other defenses against pain include the classical ego defenses, such as denial and projection, as summarized in Table A.1 in the Appendix on page 263. I see core issues also as both defenses against emotional pain and that they are commonly interwoven with the classical ego defenses.

importance of the healing power of working through them).

FIGURE 1.1. THE CHILD GOES INTO HIDING

messages from impactful relationships "The Split"

To rediscover our true or Real Self and heal our Child Within (i.e., lessen our mental, emotional, physical and relationship pain), we can begin a process that involves the following four actions that include these core issues.

1. Discover and practice being our *Real Self* or *Child Within* (sometimes not spelled with caps) as described in Chapters 5 and 6.
2. Identify our ongoing physical, mental-emotional and spiritual *needs*. Practice getting these needs met with safe and supportive people, as I address throughout this book and on page 296 in the Appendix.
3. Identify, re-experience and *grieve* the pain of our ungrieved hurts, losses or traumas in the presence of safe and supportive people.
4. Identify and work through our *core* recovery *issues*.

These four actions are closely related, and I address each one in some detail throughout this book. Working on them, and thereby healing our Child Within, generally occurs in a circular fashion, with work and discovery in one area often being a link to another area.

THE 15 CORE ISSUES

An issue is any conflict, concern or potential problem, whether conscious or unconscious, that is incomplete for us or needs action or change. A *core* issue is one that *comes up repeatedly*. We may commonly and unknowingly repeat it so often that it interferes with our day-to-day functioning in our *inner* life and our *outer* life (relationships with our family, friends, others—on or off the job, and elsewhere) and that as a result we are too often in conflict, tense and not at peace.

Our *inner life* includes our: **beliefs, thoughts, feelings, choices, decisions** and **experiences**. It also includes our **wants, needs, memories, sensations, intuitions,** and **unconscious experiences**.

There are at least 15 common core issues in relationships, recovery and living that we can recognize, name and work through. Eight of them have been described by various clinicians and authors [19,32,40] and I have added the rest. These include:

- Control
- Trust
- Being real
- Feelings
- Low self-esteem/shame
- Dependence
- Fear of abandonment
- All-or-none thinking and behaving
- High tolerance for inappropriate behavior
- Over-responsibility for others
- Neglecting my own needs
- Grieving my ungrieved hurts, losses and traumas
- Difficulty resolving conflict
- Difficulty giving love, and difficulty receiving love

At first it may not be clear just which one or perhaps more of these core issues may be involved for us. Core issues do not usually present themselves to us as an "issue." Rather, they present at first as problems in our everyday life. As problems, concerns, conflicts or painful patterns come up for us, we can share them with selected safe and supportive people. As we persistently consider and tell our story to safe others it will generally become clear just which issue or issues are involved. This knowledge will be helpful in our gradually getting free of their associated confusion, discontent, and unconscious negative life patterns (repetition compulsions or re-enactments). Throughout this book I will address and describe each of these core issues.

In the section below I introduce using some experiential aids in healing around core issues.

USING EXPERIENTIAL AIDS TO WORK THROUGH CORE ISSUES

To start working on resolving an issue includes using any one or more of the many experiential aids or techniques described in this book and in *A Gift to Myself*. Some basic principles of using these *experiential techniques* include four characteristics: 1) being *Real*, 2) being *Focused* on our Inner Life, 3) being *Structured* and 4) doing our healing work by using them in a *Safe* environment. We can use these four characteristics to assist us in working through each of our core issues over as much time as it may take. Here is a first exercise.

Experiential exercise 1: Look over the list of 15 Core Issues above. Might any of these apply in any way to any aspect of your life? (Doing these exercises now or ever is optional.)

To assist in answering, it may be helpful to turn to Table A.2 on page 265 in the Appendix and review parts of *the Core Issues Recovery Potential Survey.* Answering the items in this survey may help uncover some of these core issues and also may help indicate how important each may be in our life.

Which of these core issues tend to affect me the most? Use the survey checklist in Table A.3 in the Appendix to help you identify some of your potential or real core issues.

After you have done all that, use the space below to write each core recovery issue in the order that it has most meaning for you in your life. Place a number next to each in order of its priority, with a 1 meaning the most. List the 3 core issues that have the most meaning to you in the spaces below or on a blank page.

2   CORE ISSUE CHARACTERISTICS & DYNAMICS

HOW THEY DEVELOP

These core issues tend to emerge especially from several areas of our recovery and life:

1. Relationships – of any kind – with others, our self, and our Higher Power
2. Insight from reading, listening, reflecting upon or working through our life conflicts
3. Feedback given by our therapy group members, therapists, sponsors, friends and others
4. Doing **experiential recovery work** – throughout our healing

Recognizing, naming and working through core issues can thus assist us in describing and framing some of the origins and dynamics of such common concepts as our:

1. Problems in living
2. Day to day conflicts
3. "Character defects"
(see Step Four of the Twelve Steps) and,
4. Our struggle with our ego or false self.

When we are struggling with a particular problem or conflict, knowing about using a core-issues approach to healing will often facilitate our eventually applying a name to one or more specific issues. We *name* the issue. Once we name an issue, we can then begin to *focus* on more of the *essentials* of our particular struggle in and around the issue.

Once focused, we are less and less distracted by nonessentials and can thus *concentrate* on working to resolve these issues one at a time. As we name and work through a core issue, it can be most helpful to address it in a series of steps or stages.

WORKING THROUGH A PROBLEM, CONFLICT, OR ISSUE

1. Identify and name my specific upset, problem or conflict.

2. Reflect upon it from my powerful inner life.

3. Talk about it with safe people (i.e., tell them that specific part of my story).

4. Ask for feedback from them.

5. Name the core issue.

6. Talk about it some more.

7. Ask for some more feedback.

8. Select an appropriate experiential technique if available, or create one.

9. Use that to work on your specific conflict and feelings at a deeper level.

10. Talk or write some more about it.

11. Meditate upon it or pray about it.

12. Consider how I might learn from it

13. If I still feel incomplete, repeat any of the above.

14. Whenever I am ready, let it go.

There are several common characteristics and principles of core issues that are useful to know about in our healing.

COMMON CHARACTERISTICS

These core issues have several characteristics that we can usually discover over the time of our recovery as we learn to accept what we can and cannot change about our relationships with people, places and things. What results is what we can call wisdom to know the difference among our issues, dynamics and conflicts —which I will describe throughout this book.

As a result of being repeatedly abused and/or neglected, we are taught and learn the wrong skills to handle and deal with our day to day conflicts in our relationships. But *what we learn*, we can *un*learn. In my long clinical experience I have observed this process of learning and unlearning about these wrong life skills—which we can also call "recovery."

In assisting these many people during their recovery work, I have noticed 12 common characteristics among these core issues, as summarized in Table 2.1. Next to each of these in the Table I summarize how each characteristic relates overall to core issues.

Take a few minutes reading over and studying each of these twelve characteristics of core issues.

Bringing a core issue into our conscious awareness gives us the opportunity to complete our unfinished business around it, a better psycho-spiritual understanding of what happened then and where we are now, and a movement to self actualization, integration, wholeness, and eventual peace and serenity.

Although you may have completed the experiential exercise above, it can be hard to decide which core issue is the most important, primary, meaningful, influential or pivotal. Might it be that of needing to be in control?

Fear of abandonment? All-or-none thinking or behaving? Or some other core issue?

TABLE 2.1 TWELVE COMMON CHARACTERISTICS AMONG CORE RECOVERY ISSUES

CHARACTERISTIC	DESCRIPTION
1 **Survival Oriented**	Abused & neglected, we learn to use core issues to help us survive the associated emotional pain
2 **Defense against emotional pain**	We use one or more core issues to avoid experiencing the emotional pain, including from a current or past conflict
3 **Unconscious**	We are usually unaware or unconscious of the full dynamics involved & what is transpiring when we are involved in a core issue
4 **Primitive**	Core issues usually have a primitive or primary process nature (e.g., are dream-like, primal, & sometimes irrational). They also often have opposites (e.g., trust v distrust)
5 **Dissociation or Age-regression**	When experiencing a core issue we commonly dissociate (separate) from our full awareness of what is happening, we often dissociate & age-regress

---

CHARACTERISTIC	DESCRIPTION
6 **Ego-based**	In a core issue, our ego (false self) usually plays a major role. These dynamics are often manifested by being a martyr or a victim & by repetition compulsions (making repeated similar mistakes)
7 **Blocks Real Self awareness**	All of the above dynamics usually block our full awareness of our Real Self
8 **Often involve basic dynamics**	Core issues often involve & interact with *basic dynamics* in relationships (chapter 22) Focusing on a core issue sets in motion a flow to other issues —both core & non-core
9 **Character defects**	Core issues commonly make up a large part of our "character defects" from a Fourth Step perspective (of the Twelve Steps)
10 **Naming them can be freeing**	Like many truths in healing & recovery, naming a core issue accurately can empower us & help us heal. It is then useful to explore how the issue came to be & how it still manifests in our life

---

CHARACTERISTIC	DESCRIPTION
11 **Help in grieving**	In working through the core issues, as we grieve, we connect the pain (of experiencing the dynamics-in-action that the core issue exposes) to how we were mistreated & how our True Self went into hiding
12 **Help in all our relationships**	Most issues that we have with others, we also have with our self & with our Higher Power

CORE ISSUES AND SCHEMAS

There is a similarity between core issues and what psychologist Jeffrey Young calls Schemas. While each core issue may not have a rigid link with each specific schema, there is an overlap and psychodynamic relationship between the two. Schema therapist John Louis points out connections between schemas and core issues that can be used as a reference for each clinical truth to support one another, as shown in Table A.5 on page 276 in the Appendix. [80]

*   *   *

Because needing to be in control is such a common and pervasive issue for so many of us, I will address it next in some detail.

3   NEEDING TO BE IN CONTROL

Control may be the most dominant issue in our lives. No matter what we think we have to control—whether someone else's behavior, our own painful feelings or behavior or something else—our false self tends to latch on to this notion and won't let go. No matter if we try to control all sorts of people, places and things (PP&Ts), from alcohol, other drugs, food to gambling or sex, our ego/false self demands to be right, in control, and get its way even though allowing that may drag us down. The result is often bothersome emotional pain, confusion and frustration.

Another word for control is attachment. Wise people see attachment or needing to be in control as the basis for suffering. Is our continued suffering necessary?   We suffer when we resist what is. We all may have to suffer before we can begin to consider our alternatives. Suffering may point out the path toward peace of mind and body. One alternative that nearly always relieves our suffering is letting go: we let go of our attachment to our ego/false self, and surrender our attachment to the notion that we can control anything. We can begin to feel peace when we stop resisting what is. But doing that usually takes some work over time.

Looking again at the Serenity Prayer –

> *God grant me the serenity*
> *To accept the things I cannot change;*
> *Courage to change the things I can;*
> *And wisdom to know the difference.*

Here, the two middle lines address control as a core concern. It may come down to this wisdom—learning what I can change and what I cannot. I summarize this potential wisdom in Table 3.1 below.

Basically, I can change much of what I have some power over, such as *my inner life* (items 1 through 15 in the bottom half of Table 3.1) and *my behavior* (item 16). Although that is a lot to be responsible for, that's about *all that I can control*. These are the few things that I can muster up the courage to change most successfully.

For just about everything else, I am powerless. I cannot change them. Sometimes I may wish that I could, but ultimately I have to accept that I cannot change or control them.

When I am tempted to change any of them, I can call on the first of the Twelve Steps: "We admitted we were powerless over fill-in-the-blank and that our life had become unmanageable."

TABLE 3.1. WHAT I CAN AND CANNOT CHANGE

Accept, CANNOT Change **(I am powerless over)**	1. That I will have, and have to work through, painful feelings – necessary ones.
	2. My family (family of origin & current family)
	3. Relationships – others' beliefs, attitudes, thoughts, feelings, decisions, choices & behavior
	4. Others' differences from me
	5. My differences from others
	6. My own mistakes
	7. That I have healthy human needs
	8. My human condition
	9. That I will experience change, conflict, and duality
	10. My uniqueness and sameness as a spiritual being
Courage, I CAN Change	1. My awareness of my inner life
	2. My beliefs and attitudes
	3. My thoughts
	4. My painful feelings –necessary ones (can work through)
	5. My painful feelings –unnecessary ones (can let go)
	6. My inflated feelings
	7. My negative ego
	8. Relationships –*my* feelings, choices and behavior
	9. Getting my needs met *...cont'd next page*

Courage, I CAN Change (Cont'd)	10. My decisions and choices
	11. My expectations
	12. My martyr/victim stance
	13. Who runs my life (as a Co-creator)
	14. That I work through the conflict and duality I experience
	15. My attachment to many things, including my unnecessary suffering, my character defects, and my negative ego
	16. My behavior

I am powerless over people, places and things. I cannot control them, as summarized in items 1 through 10 at the top half of the Table.

In review: We suffer when we resist what is. We slowly find that one of the most powerful and healing acts is giving up our need to be always in control. This freedom is that of our True Self letting go of trying to change or control some people, places and things as they are, also referred to as "what is," as the Serenity Prayer suggests. In this context, the term "let go" or "surrender" does not mean to "give up" or to "lie down" in the military sense of losing a war. Rather, we mean that one who surrenders wins the struggle of trying to control, and ameliorates most of their resultant needless suffering. [104] This becomes an ongoing *process* in life, not a goal to be achieved only once.

Needing to be in control is intimately related to and includes several other major life issues: willpower, fear of losing control, dependence/ independence, trust, experiencing feelings, especially anger, self-esteem and shame, being spontaneous, self-nurturing, all-or-none and expectations of self and others.

Many of us may not have worked through these important life issues. However, we may believe that we have overcome, i.e., controlled these issues and all of our other life problems. We may even believe we can somehow control life itself.

Ultimately, we cannot control life. The more that we try to control it, the more out of control we often feel because we are focusing so much attention on it. Often the person who *feels out* of control is obsessed with the need to *be in* control. It is hard to learn that life cannot be controlled. Life's powerful and mysterious process goes on, no matter what we do. Life cannot be controlled because it is far too rich, spontaneous and rambunctious to be fully understood, much less controlled by our thinking, controlling ego/false self. [15,17,18]

At this point we can discover that there is a way out, a way to get free of the suffering associated with our always needing to be in control. The way out is to let go and let God, surrender, and then to become, gradually, a co-creator of our life. This is where the spiritual aspect of recovery comes into play as a powerful aid. Attendance at and working Twelve Step recovery programs such as Al-Anon, Alcoholics Anonymous, Narcotics Anonymous, ACA/ACoA, CoDA, Emotions Anonymous and Overeaters Anonymous and others are helpful. Other spiritual paths may also help.

We work on our control issues by asking for help from appropriate others and by letting go of our ego and our attachment to it. [101, 102] When we do this, we begin to discover our True Self, and we begin to feel more alive.

HEALTHY ASPECTS OF CONTROL

The normal or healthy side of control is when we use it for practical purposes that help us to be responsible for our own well being. This well being includes the realms of our mental, emotional, physical, financial and relationship wants, needs and issues. To control our self in this way—as opposed to trying to control others—is positive, healthy, constructive, responsible, and creative. We can control only our own inner life and what we personally do with others in our outer life. How we thus process our own thoughts and feelings and what we do with these is the only way to get lasting peace. When we experience a new conflict it becomes an opportunity to see once again how to renegotiate conflict in our inner life. Some define control as the ability to purposefully direct, or suppress, change. But that definition usually works only when we apply it as outlined here.

More on healthy control: Psychologist Abraham Maslow described a hierarchy of human needs. He said that when we do not take responsibility for getting our lower level needs met, then we will be unlikely to get our higher-level needs met—until we first meet our lower needs. Study this diagram carefully (Figure 3). A positive way to get our needs met will be to begin a full recovery program for whatever stage in which we may be, as shown beside Maslow's needs hierarchy figure. (For a summary on neglecting my own needs see Section A.5 on page 296 in the Appendix.)

We don't need to be "in control" all of the time. What we may actually have is a *sense* of control. When our parents or bosses are "controlling" us, we can accept that because we **trust** them to provide *not complete* control of our life a management-based action on their appropriate goals, caring, rules, monitoring and feedback that we realistically seek and appreciate. Many of us actively seek parent-figures or mentors who will provide this special kind of guidance and control.

Figure 3. Maslow's Hierarchy of Needs ↔ Recovery, Prevention and Maintenance

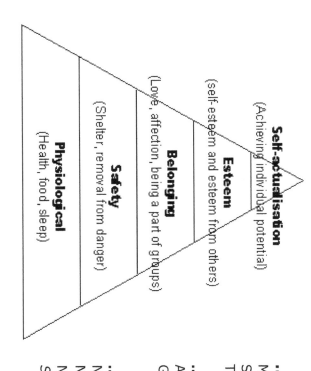

Self-actualisation
(Achieving individual potential)

Esteem
(self-esteem and esteem from others)

Belonging
(Love, affection, being a part of groups)

Safety
(Shelter, removal from danger)

Physiological
(Health, food, sleep)

··· Stage 3 Program (pages 205, 275)
Meditation, prayer, spiritual literature
Study *A Course in Miracles*
Twelve Step work – useful in all stages

···Stage 2 Recovery Program
ACA, CoDA, 1:1 Counseling,
Group therapy, Bibliotherapy

··· Stage 1 Recovery Program- *Begin*
No tobacco or other toxic drug use.
No other high-risk behaviors.
No overeating. Twelve Step work.
See Table A.4 on page 270 for more.

When we seek their advice and comply with or follow them in a spirit of co-commitment, we are depending on them to help us strengthen what we *can* control. We give up control to gain control of our freedom and creativity through their knowledge, experience and wisdom. We describe this process via several examples in our book *The Power of Humility*. [100]

So the up side of control is using it to make our inner life better and to give us peace, to allow us to experience the peace that is already and always in us as us.

The down side is that trying to control people, places and things outside of our real mental, emotional and physical self so much ends up being to our detriment. The unhealthy side of needing to be in control comes not from our real self but from our false self or ego. Our ego wants to be *in control* and *right* all the time that we will let it. The best description of the ego is not from Freud or any of his colleagues, although they did begin to address it. In my experience the most detailed and accurate treatise on the ego is in the modern spiritual text *A Course in Miracles,* which I address below.

LETTING GO OF CONTROL

We work on control by —

1. *naming* it when we find it as a current issue, and then practicing -
2. *letting it go,* and if open to it
3. asking for *help from* appropriate *safe others* such as a therapist, counselor, sponsor or the like.

When we do this, we begin to discover our Real Self and begin to feel more alive. (This 3-part principle works for most of the other core issues. See page 10 for a detailed breakdown of these 3 principles.) In Table 3.2 below I summarize seven paths or recovery aids for letting go of *needing to be in* control. Take a minute and look over this table's contents. Look at each path/aid to letting go and the key terms and comments next to each. A focus of nearly all of them is by living in what a generic or broad-based spirituality calls the Eternal Now. You may have already looked into one or more of these, and may be well familiar with some. Some example descriptions follow.

The First Step of the Fellowship of Alcoholics Anonymous addresses control directly:

WE ADMITTED WE WERE POWERLESS OVER

FILL-IN-THE-BLANK_____,

—THAT OUR LIVES HAD BECOME UNMANAGEABLE.

TABLE 3.2. PATHS TO LETTING GO OF [NEEDING TO BE IN] **CONTROL BY LIVING IN THE NOW**

Working Recovery Aids	Key Terms	Comments
1 Twelve Steps of AA & other fellowships	Let go [of ego], & let God	To work the Steps it usually helps to be in the Now, & let go/surrender
2 Generic Spirituality	Eternal Now	From the perennial philosophy that is part of, yet transcends, world religions
3 *A Course in Miracles*	Holy Instant	Sophisticated & effective handbook on ego psychology. Teaches simple prayer as a way out of conflict. Be at peace Now.
4 Ram Dass' teachings	Be Here Now	The 'truth' in this three-word title of his 1971 book
5 Eckhart Tolle teachings	The Power of Now	Let go of ego/false self into the power & peace of Now
6 Abraham-Hicks' teachings	More descriptions of Now	Simple, yet sophisticated advice for spiritual seekers
7 Power of Humility book	How *Now* fits with humility	Teaches how to use humility in relationships Now

In so many words it says, "I'm not in control. I am not in charge. I am indeed powerless over whatever I'm clinging to—whatever I'm attached to in an unhealthy way." The basis for needing to be in control is our attachment to our false self, to our ego, or negative ego. AA'ers also call it "King Baby," and others the grandiose self or the co-dependent self. One of its characteristics is that it thinks that it is, and it behaves as though it must always be "in control." It has to be in control because that's the only way it can think it amounts to anything (which is also about another core issue—shame).

Needing to be in control is a way to defend against emotional pain. We are controlling our feelings, our emotions, what's coming up for us from our inner life. On the one hand, all of that is useful, because most of these so-called "ego defenses" have some limited usefulness. But they are double-edged swords too, because they have some detrimental or destructive qualities. And, of course, that is controlling someone or something to the extent that it ends up harming *us*—the very one who's trying to do the controlling. That's what nearly every addict and co-dependent eventually does. And it is another reason why control is a core recovery issue. [83, 103]

We might ask: Are these core issues actually ways by which we limit ourselves from realizing who we really are? AA's 4th and 5th Steps address our *character defects*—which are actually and *mostly* about our *core issues*—which started out as being our friends.

Step 4. Made a searching and fearless moral inventory of ourselves.

5. Admitted to God, to ourselves and to another human being the exact nature of our wrongs.

6. Were entirely ready to have God remove all these defects of character.

7. Humbly asked Him to remove our Shortcomings.

As defenses against emotional pain, our core issues/character defects helped us to survive in an abusive and neglectful family and world. But now, when we get closer to having healthy relationships, they tend to get in the way. What we are trying to do in recovery, since we are getting into healthier relationships (and which is an important marker of recovery), is that we may want to let go of these various "defects." Before we can let go of them, we have to be not only willing, but we have to *know* what it is that we're *letting go of*. That's why I have described the importance of "getting down on the floor and wrestling with it" before I can know what it is that I am letting go. That's in part why I wrote this book.

As another example, *A Course in Miracles* (*ACIM*) says, "The ego is the wrong-minded attempt to perceive yourself as you wish to be, rather than as you are. Yet you can know yourself only as you are, because that is all you can be sure of." As I have referred to it in *Healing the Child Within*, the ego is the false self, and by contrast "...as you are," and "...all you can be sure of "is the True or Real Self, which can also be called the Child Within, Soul or Human Heart, as it is connected to God, and which the Course calls *right mind*." It continues, "The ego is the questioning aspect of the post-separation self [*us* —after we thought we left God], which was made rather than created. It is capable of asking questions but not of perceiving meaningful answers, because these would involve knowledge and cannot be perceived." (*ACIM* 42T, 2:3-4).

One way to suspect that we are in our ego is if we are experiencing *tension, fear, conflict, anger, guilt* or *shame*, and at that moment, we have not chosen God. In short, if we don't feel peace, we are likely to be in or attached to our ego.

*   *   *

In the next chapter I address the second most common core issue that many of us encounter in our relationships and our recovery: all-or-none thinking and behaving.

4 ALL-OR-NONE THINKING AND BEHAVING

With needing to be in control, all-or-none thinking and behaving is also one of the first and most primitive of the core issues commonly encountered in any stage of recovery. It limits my possibilities and choices because it says that all I can want or get in any relationship with a person, place or thing is "all *or* none." Either a zero or a ten—nowhere in between. But how often *have* I or *do* I ever get "all"? If I get "all" rarely or never, then what does that leave? *None.* So with an all-or-none mindset, I may end up believing or feeling that I essentially have *no* choices.

We get stuck in all-or-none thinking and behaving when we remain attached to our ego/false self. The false self can make only walls, not healthy boundaries. Walls tend to alienate others, in contrast to assertive healthy boundaries that often work better to get what we want. As I begin to live from and as my True Self, I can learn to set healthy boundaries and limits, which in turn will allow me many more choices in my life. With this new insight and understanding I can choose among any one or more of the many points along the many spaces across the all-or-none spectrum from zero to ten.

All-or-none is the ego defense against pain that therapists call *splitting*. When we think or act this way, we do so at either one extreme or the other. For example, either we love someone completely or we hate them. There is no middle ground. (This core issue is so ingrained into a part of our collective unconscious that I found some 24 published songs about it, such as in the musical *Oklahoma* "With me, it's all or nothing…" and in another popular song "All, or nothing at all"). We see the people around us as either good or bad, and not the real composite they are. We judge *ourselves* equally as harshly. The more we use all-or-none *thinking*, the more it opens us up to *behaving* in an all-or-none fashion. Both of these actions tend to get us into trouble and to cause us to suffer unnecessarily.

We may become attracted to others who think and behave in an all-or-none fashion. But being around this kind of person tends to result in more trouble and pain for us. We may have been attracted to them because our *parents* may have *modeled it* for us along with other kinds of family dysfunction. While all-or-none thinking can occur in any of these family situations, it can stereotypically occur for example often among fundamentalist religious parents. They are often rigid, punitive, judgmental, and perfectionistic. They are often in a shame-based system, which attempts to cover over and even silence our True Self.

All-or-none thinking is similar to active alcoholism, other chemical dependence, co-dependence or other active addictions and attachments, in that it sharply and unrealistically *limits* our possibilities and *choices*. To be so limited makes us feel constricted, and we are unable to be creative and to grow in our day-to-day lives.

In recovery, we begin to learn that most things in our life, including our recovery, are not all-or-none. They are not either/or. Rather, they are often parts of both/and. They have shades of gray, they are somewhere along the spectrum of the middle, a 3, 4, 5, 6, or 7 and not either a 0 or a 10.

All-or-none has several guises, manifestations or variations described in the psychology literature—as I summarize in Table 4.1. Psychologists call these kinds of unhealthy thinking "cognitive distortions" (errors in thinking). [23] And they call learning to *handle* and ultimately *let go* of these irrational defenses against pain by the term "cognitive restructuring" (cognitive is psych-speak for thinking, often expanded to include emotions and behavior). [24] Read over and, if interested, study each of these guises of all-or-none. These 11 ways of seeing and further describing it expands our understanding of this second most encountered core issue that emerge in relationship conflicts and early in the process of recovery.

TABLE 4.1. GUISES AND DIMENSIONS OF ALL-OR-NONE [23]

Guise of All-or-None	Definition	Comment
All-or-None	Absolute terms, like "always", "every", "never", and "there is no alternative"	Few aspects of human behavior are so absolute
Splitting	Thinking and acting in extremes (e.g., good v bad, powerful v defenseless, etc).	Can be seen as a developmental stage *and* an ego defense
Overgeneralizing	Using isolated cases to generalize widely	Limits our choices and our freedom
Mentally filters out the positive	Almost exclusive focus on negative aspects of something while ignoring the positive.	e.g., focusing on a tiny imperfection in a piece of otherwise useful clothing
Disqualifying the positive	Continually deemphasizing or declining the positive for arbitrary, *ad hoc* reasons	*ad hoc* ("for this purpose") = task oriented

TABLE 4.1. GUISES AND DIMENSIONS OF ALL-OR-NONE (*CONTINUED*)

Guise of All-or-None	Definition	Comment
Jumping to conclusions	Drawing negative conclusions from little or no evidence. Subtypes: 1) *Mind reading* -Assuming special knowledge of the intentions or thoughts of others and ...	2) *Fortune telling* – Exaggerating how things will turn out before they happen.
Magnifying and minimizing	Distorting aspects of a memory or situation through magnifying or minimizing them such that they no longer correspond to objective reality. "Making a mountain out of a molehill"	A subtype: *Catastrophizing* – Focusing on worst possible outcome (however unlikely) or thinking a situation is unbearable or impossible when it is really just uncomfortable
Emotional reasoning	Making decisions & arguments based on intuitions or on a *feeling* v. objective evidence	"I rely on my intuition or feelings too often"

TABLE 4.1. GUISES AND DIMENSIONS OF ALL-OR-NONE (*END*)

Guise of All-or-None	Definition	Comment
"Shoulding" **on self** **thinking or** **statements**	Thinking things "should" or "ought" to be rather than the actual situation we are faced with, or having ...	...rigid rules which we believe will "always apply" no matter what the circumstances
Labeling **and** *mis*label-**ing**	Explaining PPTs merely by naming them; related to overgeneralization. Rather than describing the specific behavior, assigns a label to someone that implies absolute and unalterable terms	*Mis*labeling is describing a PPT with exaggerated, highly colored and emotionally loaded language
Personali-zation	Attribution of responsibility or causal role for events over which we have no control	May be used to blame others

PPT = Person, place or thing

The next time or two you find yourself painfully conflicted over *anything*, ask yourself if a core issue may be involved. If it involves all-or-none thinking and behaving, now that you understand what it is, how would you approach it? In the space below, briefly describe how you would now handle such a situation.

_____

_____

_____

_____

_____

_____

_____

_____

_____

Note: I address our healthy human needs in various ways as they relate to various core issues throughout this book (see **Index**). To supplement this I include a brief summary of the core issue of neglecting my own needs in **Section A.5** on page 296 of the **Appendix**, and thus I will not include a separate chapter on it in the text.

To handle any conflict—including a core issue—it usually works best if we are functioning *as* and *from* our Real Self (True Self, Core Self, Child Within). I have described it throughout several of my prior books, and will now review its essentials in the next two chapters.

5 BEING REAL - IDENTIFYING OUR REAL SELF

Being real is key among all the other core issues. It is the lynch-pin to recognizing, working through and getting free of the pain that getting stuck in them promotes. Study this section if you have time and want to free yourself of unnecessary emotional and much physical pain. Here is what I know about it.

In my book *Healing the Child Within* I used several terms interchangeably: Real Self, True Self, Child Within, Inner Child, Divine Child, and Higher Self. (Although caps are not necessary, I capitalize the first letters to show its importance for us in living and to help differentiate it from the false self.) It has also been called our Deepest Self, our Inner Core. [52] Each of these terms refers to the same core part of us, which is who we are when we feel most authentic, genuine or spirited.

OUR REAL SELF

Our Real Self is our true identity. It is who we really are. It is spontaneous, expansive, loving, giving, and communicating. It accepts ourselves and others. It feels, whether the feelings may be joyful or painful. [And it expresses those feelings when appropriate] Our Real Self accepts our feelings without judgment and fear, and allows them to exist as a valid way of accessing and appreciating life's events. (If reading this description is slow for you at any time, consider looking over the differences between the real and false self in Table 5.1 on the next page).

Our Child Within is expressive, assertive, and creative. It can be childlike in the highest, most mature, and evolved sense of the word. It needs to play and to have fun. And yet it is vulnerable, perhaps because it is so open and trusting. It surrenders to itself, to others and ultimately to the God of our understanding. And yet it is powerful in the true sense of power (discussed in Chapters 11 and 15). It is healthily self-indulgent, taking pleasure in receiving and in being nurtured. It is also open to that vast and mysterious part of us that we call our unconscious. It pays attention to the messages that we receive daily from our unconscious, such as dreams, struggles and illness.

By being real, it is free to grow. And while our false self forgets, our Real Self remembers our Oneness with others and with the Universe. Yet for most of us our Real Self is also our private self.

TABLE 5.1. SOME CHARACTERISTICS OF OUR REAL SELF AND FALSE SELF [66, 68, 91]

Real Self	False Self
Authentic, True Self	Unauthentic self, mask, persona, ego
Genuine	Un-genuine, "as-if" personality
Spontaneous	Plans, plods or impulsive
Expansive, loving	Contracting, fearful
Giving, communicating	Withholding
Accepting of self and others	Envious, critical, idealizes, perfectionistic
Compassionate	Other-oriented, conforming, co-dependent
Loves Unconditionally	Loves conditionally
Feels feelings, including appropriate spontaneous, current anger	Denies or hides feelings, including long-held anger (resentment)
Assertive	Aggressive and/or passive
Child Within, Inner Child	Over-developed parent/adult scripts;
Ability to be child-like	may be childish
Needs to play and have fun	Avoids play and fun
Vulnerable	Pretends always to be strong
Powerful in true sense	Gives power away
Trusting	Distrusting
Enjoys being nurtured	Avoids being nurtured
Surrenders	Controls, withdraws
Self caring/indulgent	Self-righteous

--- continued on next page

Real Self	False Self
Openness, willing to learn	Arrogant
Remembers our Oneness	Forgets our Oneness; feels separate
Free to grow	Tends to act out unconscious painful patterns
Private self	Public self

Who knows why we chose not to share? Perhaps it is a fear of being hurt or being rejected. Some have estimated that we show our True Self to others on average for only about 15 minutes each day. For whatever reasons, we tend to keep that part of us private.

When we "come from" or when we *are* our True Self, we feel alive. We may feel pain in the form of hurt, sadness, guilt or anger, but we nonetheless feel alive. Or we may feel joy, in the form of contentment, happiness, inspiration or even ecstasy. Overall, we tend to feel current, complete, finished, appropriate, real, whole and sane.

Our Child Within flows naturally from the time we are born to the time that we die and during all of our times and transitions in between. We don't have to do anything to be our True Self. It just is. If we simply let it be, it will express itself with no particular effort on our part.

Indeed, any effort is usually in denying our awareness and expression of it. [66, 68, 91]

OUR FALSE SELF OR EGO

By contrast, another part of us generally feels uncomfortable, strained, or unauthentic. I use the following terms interchangeably: false self, ego, co-dependent self, unauthentic or public self.

Our false self is a cover-up. It is inhibited, contracting and fearful. It is our egocentric ego and super-ego, forever planning and plodding, continually selfish and withholding. It is envious, critical, idealized, blaming, shaming and perfectionistic.

Alienated from the True Self, our false self is other-oriented, it focuses on what it thinks others want it to be; it is over-conforming, and too often "politically correct" to our detriment . It gives its love only conditionally. It covers up, hides or denies feelings. Even so, it may make up false feelings, as it often does when we consistently answer a "How are you?" with a perfunctory "I'm just fine." This quick response is often necessary or helpful to defend against the frightening awareness of the false self, which either doesn't know how it feels or does know and has censured these feelings as "wrong," or "bad."

Rather than be appropriately assertive—for the Real Self—it is often either inappropriately aggressive and/or passive. Our false self tends to be the "critical parent" —should we use transactional analysis script terminology. It avoids playing and having fun. It pretends to be "strong" or even "powerful." Yet its power is only minimal or nonexistent, and it is in reality usually fearful, distrusting and destructive.

Because our false self needs to withdraw and to be in control, it sacrifices nurturing or being nurtured. It cannot surrender. It is self-righteous and attempts to block information coming from the unconscious. Even so, it tends to repeatedly act out unconscious, often painful patterns. Because it forgets our Oneness, it feels separate. It is our public self—who we think others and eventually even we think we should be.

Most of the time, when we are in the role of our false self, we feel uncomfortable, numb, empty or in a contrived or contracted state. We do not feel real, complete, whole or sane. At one level or another, we sense that something is wrong, and that something is missing.

Paradoxically, we often feel like this false self is our natural state, the way we "should be." This could be our addiction or attachment to being that way. We become so accustomed to being our false self that our Real Self feels guilty, like something is wrong, that we shouldn't feel real and alive. To consider changing this problem is frightening.

This false or co-dependent self appears to be universal among humans. It has been described or referred to countless times in print and in our daily lives. It has been called such diverse names as a survival tool, psychopathology, the egocentric ego and the impaired or defensive self. [66] It can be destructive to self, others and intimate relationships. It is a double-edged sword. It has some uses. But just how useful is it? And under what circumstances? The following poem by Charles C. Finn describes many of our struggles with our false self.

PLEASE HEAR WHAT I'M NOT SAYING

Don 't be fooled by me.

Don't be fooled by the face I wear.

For I wear a mask, a thousand masks, masks that I'm afraid to take off, and none of them is me.

Pretending is an art that's second nature with me. but don't be fooled.

For God's sake don't be fooled.

I give you the impression that I'm secure, that all is sunny and unruffled with me, within as well as without, that confidence is my name and coolness my game, that the water's calm and I'm in command, and that I need no one.

But don't believe me.

My surface may seem smooth but my surface is my mask, ever-varying and ever-concealing.

Beneath lies no complacence. Beneath lies confusion and fear and aloneness.

But I hide this. I don't want anybody to know it.

I panic at the thought of my weakness and fear being exposed. That's why I frantically create a mask to hide behind, a nonchalant sophisticated facade, to help me pretend, to shield me from the glance that knows.

But such a glance is precisely my salvation. My only hope and I know it. That is, if it's followed by acceptance, if it's followed by love.

It's the only thing that can liberate me from myself, from my own self-built prison walls, from the barriers I so painstakingly erect.

It's the only thing that will assure me of what I can't assure myself, that I'm really worth something.

But I don't tell you this. I don't dare. I'm afraid to. I'm afraid your glance will not be followed by acceptance, will not be followed by love.

I'm afraid you'll think less of me, that you'll laugh, and your laugh would kill me.

Wisdom to Know The Difference

I'm afraid that deep-down I'm nothing, that I'm just no good, and that you will see this and reject me.

So I play my game, my desperate pretending game, with a facade of assurance without and a trembling child within.

So begins the glittering but empty parade of masks, and my life becomes a front.

I idly chatter to you in the suave tones of surface talk. I tell you everything that's really nothing, and nothing of what's everything, of what's crying within me.

So when I'm going through my routine, do not be fooled by what I'm saying.

Please listen carefully and try to hear what I'm not saying, what I'd like to be able to say, what for survival I need to say, but what I can't say.

I don't like to hide. I don't like to play superficial phony games. I want to stop playing them.

I want to be genuine and spontaneous and me, but you've got to help me.

You've got to hold out your hand even when that's the last thing I seem to want.

Only you can wipe away from my eyes the blank stare of the breathing dead. Only you can call me into aliveness.

Each time you're kind and gentle and encouraging, each time you try to understand because you really care, my heart begins to grow wings, very small wings, very feeble wings, but wings!

With your power to touch me into feeling you can breathe life into me.

I want you to know that.

I want you to know how important you are to me, how you can be a creator—a honest-to-God creator— of the person that is me if you choose to.

You alone can break down the wall behind which I tremble, you alone can remove my mask, you alone can release me from my shadow-world of panic and uncertainty, from my lonely prison, if you choose to.

Please choose to. Do not pass me by. It will not be easy for you.

A long conviction of worthlessness builds strong walls. The nearer you approach to me the blinder I may strike back.

It's irrational, but despite what the books say about man, often I am irrational.

I fight against the very thing that I cry out for. But I am told that love is stronger than strong walls, and in this lies my hope.

Please try to beat down those walls with firm hands but with gentle hands for a child is very sensitive.

Who am I, you may wonder? I am someone you know very well.

For I am every man you meet and
I am every woman you meet.

—Charles C. Finn

RISKING BEING REAL

What was it like for you to read the poem above? I may have trusted some people in my past and they ended up hurting me. So how can I really tell? My experience is that there is no 100% sure way to tell without experimenting, using trial and error or a share-check-share approach.

To risk being real with people takes *courage, motivation, awareness* and the *discernment* to seek out and find *safe* others. To do that is not always easy. It takes practice and trial and error. On the next page I list some key characteristics of safe people compared to unsafe ones. Look this over carefully.

Not all of these safe/unsafe characteristics are absolute. For example, some people who make eye contact, appear to listen to you and are at times supportive may *still* be unsafe. And a safe person may be unclear at times. But, over time, these characteristics may be helpful in differentiating who is safe from who is unsafe.

TABLE 5.2 SOME CHARACTERISTICS OF SAFE AND UNSAFE PEOPLE [92]

Safe	Unsafe
• Listen to you	• Don't listen
• Hear you	• Don't hear
• Make eye contact	• No eye contact
• Accept the real you	• Reject the real you
• Validate the real you	• Invalidate the real you
• Non-judgmental	• Judgmental
• Are real with you	• False with you
• Clear	• Unclear
• Boundaries appropriate and clear	• Boundaries unclear, messages mixed
• Direct	• Indirect
• No triangles	• Triangle-in others
• Supportive	• Competitive
• Loyal	• Betray
• Relationship authentic	• Relationship feels contrived

Have you *met* anyone who feels safe to you?

Do you *know* anyone *now* who feels safe?

Has it been scary or difficult for you to find safe people? YES

If you have a few minutes, reflect on who you knew in the past and who you know now. Include anyone who comes up in your awareness. Of these people, who has felt safe—or *feels* safe to you now. In the space below write in either the names, initials, description or a code word for anyone who felt or feels safe to you now. Remember, this is your private journal, so what you write in it is for your eyes only.

_____
_____
_____
_____

Next, list any *un*safe people in your life in the space below. Take your time doing these experiential exercises. When you come to a point where you feel that you've about completed your list of safe people, consider the following. Pick one person on the list, perhaps the safest. Meet with them in person and tell them how and why you feel safe with them (if they are too far away, you might consider calling them.)

_____
_____

_____

_____

What was this like to do this exercise? What was it like to share what you did with your safest person? What feelings came up or are coming up for you now? In the space below write your answers to these questions, and/or write whatever is coming up for you right now. Take as much time and space as you need.

_____

_____

_____

_____

_____

PRACTICING BEING REAL

Each time that we share from and as our real self, we are practicing being real. Continue sharing whenever you think that is what you want and what is appropriate with a safe person. Examples of safe people are licensed therapists, counselors and usually Twelve Step group sponsors and most of their members, plus essentially all therapy group members. We have to find other safe people through trial and error, share-check-share, summarized below.

BEING REAL

After we practice enough over time, we have now developed the *motivation, awareness* and the *discernment* to be real most of the time. If we are in doubt with anyone or when we meet a stranger we can use a share-check-share approach. We share some of our experience or information and then check for their response to it. If their response feels safe, over time, then we share some more. Then we check again, and so on. Trial and error.

When a stress, hurt, loss or trauma occurs when we have been real with someone or when it may be associated with any other core issue—the associated stress can trigger us into an age-regression. Age regression freezes us into a state of immediate and sometimes longer loss of our full awareness and dysfunction where we can no longer make a voluntary choice to be real or not.

When we are with an unsafe person we tend to age regress more often. When that happens we can get stuck or frozen in it and feel as though we can't escape. Then we can almost never be aware of and share from our real self until we come out of the age-regressed state. Because this experience is so common, I describe it briefly in the next chapter.

6   BEING REAL – 2
THE ROLE OF AGE REGRESSION

CORE ISSUES AND AGE REGRESSION

Finding ourself *in* a core issue—swept up or caught in its conflict, confusion or distraction—can easily trigger an age regression. When a stress, hurt, loss or trauma occurs in association with any core issue—the pain can trigger us into an age-regression. When we age regress we usually feel mentally and emotionally paralyzed. When that happens we can get stuck or frozen in it and feel as though we can't escape. Because of its often and close association with core issues, I will briefly summarize what it is.

Just learning about age regression can be healing. An important reason for this is because it is often a major teacher about *being real*, most of the *other core issues* and having *healthy boundaries*.

Age regression happens when we suddenly feel upset, confused and scared, like a helpless little child. There may be no apparent cause for it, and it may last a few minutes or longer. It can feel as though one minute we are an adult, feeling okay, and in a matter of seconds we feel like an out-of-control and helpless little person. Has anything like that ever happened to you? *Oh God Yes*

We can begin to heal ourselves around such an age regression when one happens by beginning to observe our inner life and what is happening around us. As we heal our Real Self, we can discover that while it is painful and debilitating, age regression is actually a gift in disguise. For one thing, it can teach us about *boundaries*. This is because the genesis of age regression and its recurrence throughout childhood, adolescence and adulthood nearly always means the same thing. Our boundaries are being invaded, they are about to be invaded, or this particular experience that I am having right this minute is somehow reminding me of a past experience when my boundaries were invaded. A *core issue* is also often involved when we age regress. But when we are age regressed we cannot think clearly enough even to consider that possibility. But there is a way out, which I describe below.

Age regression can arise in many and various circumstances, such as when someone yells at us or shames us in some way (core issues of *shame* and *difficulty handling conflict*). These may include a comment about our looks or weight or a mistake we may have made (*shame* again). There is thus usually a trigger that initiates the rapid sequence of age regression. This trigger may be any of a number of possibilities, including any mistreatment or abandonment by anyone (*fear of abandonment*), any negative message from anyone, any form of invalidation (*difficulty trusting, difficulty handling conflict*) or anything that reminds us of any of the above.

We can age regress at any time, in any place and for any reason. Immediately after the triggering event, we may suddenly feel the following in rapid sequence: **fear**, **hurt**, **shame**, **guilt**, **anger**, **confusion** and **disorientation** (*feelings*). We may end up feeling dysfunctional and out of control, almost as if we want to scream. But our True Self feels too weak even for that, so it may want just to go back into hiding (*difficulty being real, needing to be in control, all-or-none*).

When age regression continues to wound us with no healing around it, we may remain paralyzed, confused and dysfunctional, and our True Self stays in hiding (Figure 1.2 on page 3 above). When we recognize it and heal it, age regression can be a useful opportunity in our healing and well-being. To heal it we recognize it, work through it and learn from it. To do all of this can take many months and more often several years in a full recovery program.

HEALING AGE REGRESSION

The first step in healing age regression is to *recognize* it when it happens. This is a kind of *self-diagnosis*. Visiting our *family of origin* is often an opportune time to self-diagnose age regression because we may get mistreated, mentally or emotionally abandoned or invalidated there so frequently. When it happens, I might say to myself something like, "Hey, I'm age regressing now," or "I just age regressed." This is a great moment, because when we *name it*, we can do something about it.

We can then begin to take some *slow deep breaths*. And then *walk around the room* or take a *walk outside*. (The point is not to be immobilized, since that may contribute to perpetuating our feeling of immobilization and helplessness.) Then begin to *look at various objects* in the room. Walk into another room and do the same.

We can also *pick up our keys* and begin to play with them. Keys are symbols of freedom. They open doors and start car engines. Preventing and managing the sometimes crippling effects of age regression, when convenient, we always *have a way out* of our family member's house or any other potentially toxic environment if the going gets too difficult. We can bring our car with us, stay in a motel or have some other way to get out should we need to. Doing so is a way of setting healthy boundaries so that our Real Self can begin to observe and process it all.

PROCESSING THE EXPERIENCE

As soon as possible, *talk about it* with a *safe* person. This is why, when convenient, it can be helpful to bring a safe person with us when we visit—or when an unsafe person visits us. If there is no one to talk with, perhaps we can call a friend or *write down what happened* and how it felt, and then talk it over with a safe person later. Even later we can talk about it some more. This is a great healing opportunity, and it can be most helpful to *talk it over* with our therapist, therapy group, or other safe people.

It is helpful eventually to *work through what happened* and how it felt during the age regression in a deeper and experiential way. Some techniques to facilitate this include telling our story, doing anger bat work, writing and reading (to a safe person) an unmailed letter, family sculpture, gestalt techniques and any creative technique. [92]

Then consider the **levels of meaning** that the age regression may have for us. For example:

Level 1—I was mistreated in the past.

2—I am being mistreated now.

3—I don't want to be mistreated anymore.

4—I'm going to set firm boundaries and limits in this relationship.

5—I'm going to take a break from or possibly even leave this relationship if the mistreatment continues.

6—I can get free of this unnecessary pain and suffering.

7—I consider any core issues associated with it.

8—I am learning and growing from my awareness of this age regression.

9—By using it, I am healing my True Self.

At about Level 5 above, people sometimes may feel as if they are being mistreated without looking at their own role in the mistreatment. Or they may be mistreating their partner, such as intruding on their partner's boundaries without realizing it. They may not realize how their words or behavior may be invading their partner's boundaries in a sometimes subtle way.

We recognize these triggers as they come up for us. By doing so, we can then avoid situations where we may anticipate they will happen. Finally, we can use all of the above constructively. We can begin to 1) recognize and heal any future age regressions, 2) avoid or minimize contact with people who do triggering behaviors, 3) protect our Child Within, 4) stop blaming ourself, and 5) bring the previously unconscious core issues that we encounter in our life more into our full awareness.

FURTHER MEANINGS

When approached in a conscious, self-caring way, age regressions can be healing since they get us in touch with our past unhealed hurts, losses and traumas and our core issues. We heal ourselves in this way in a safe environment. If we are continually exposed to mistreatment, we can heal an age regression in a safe place such as individual counseling, a therapy group, or a similar support group. For some people, age regressions may be associated with panic attacks, and the above steps can be helpful in handling many panic attacks.

Age regression is a sudden decompensation that is triggered by a hurt that is nearly always due to an actual or a possible boundary invasion and is often associated with one or more core issues. It occurs commonly among adult children of unhealthy families and in people with post-traumatic stress disorder (PTSD).

THREE KINDS OF
AGE REGRESSION AND PROJECTION

In recovery we discover that there are three kinds of age regression.

1) The first is the most common as described above, wherein we end up with a paralyzed or passive state and feeling.

2) The second kind may have the same triggers and feelings, but we become much more upset and active. For example, we may throw a temper tantrum, at times even verbally attacking someone close to us. Or we may express pain by crying and even some shaking or contorting of our body. This second kind is often called an *abreaction*.

3) The third type is a "therapeutic" variety of age regression, wherein either one or a combination of the above two types occurs during the normal and constructive course of group or individual therapy. When this type occurs in a safe and supportive environment, we can heal more easily, although if we are with safe others outside of a therapeutic context we can also heal to some extent.

Projection: All three of these kinds of age regression can result from and generate more conflict and thus become a part of the core issue of difficulty handling conflict. But we can use the occurrence of both the age regression and the conflict to help us go deeper into our pain and to heal. This intense feeling of conflict is a part of the phenomenon and defense against emotional pain known as *transference* or *projection*, which can be experienced in at least three situations:

1. With anyone with whom I am in current conflict.
2. With what the current conflict *reminds me of* (this is a deeper level that addresses past unfinished hurts).
3. With what old tapes or messages I may be playing in my own mind about all of this. (This is also a deeper level, and a way that I may often beat myself up).

To heal age regression, we need to have safe, close people to assist us. Learning about age regression opens doors to the richness and opportunities that lie deep within our inner life, and it helps us begin to sort out each of our core issues. While age regression. may be either dramatic or subtle, another form of boundary distortion that is usually subtle, though common, is a complex defense mechanism called *projective identification*, which I address in Chapter 6 of *Boundaries and Relationships*.

7   FEAR OF ABANDONMENT

Fear of being abandoned may be one of the most primitive and yet complicated of the core issues. It begins in our earliest time of life. Related to the core issue of trust and difficulty trusting, it is usually more visible among children who grew up in troubled families.

UNCONSCIOUS DYNAMICS

If we felt abandoned when we were young, then eventually our unconscious mind may fear any sign that we may be left alone again. Our fear can come up even if things are otherwise secure. In this way our unconscious mind may be trying to sort out current reality with our past reality. But we are now emotionally stronger to handle such a loss. Our increased fear is now unnecessary. This situation is like a bird whose cage door has been opened but that still remains trapped inside because its changed circumstances haven't really registered with its full awareness.

Some of my patients reported that their parents threatened to leave or abandon them as a disciplinary measure when they were infants and young children. This is a cruelty and trauma that may appear benign to some on the surface, although in my opinion it is a covert form of child abuse.

John was a 34-year-old divorced man, a successful writer, who grew up in a troubled and dysfunctional family. He told us in group, "I can't remember much about my life before age 5, but at that time my father left me, my mother and my younger sister out of the blue! He had told my mother he had a job to do out West and would be back. But he didn't tell us kids. And what's more, my mother shipped me off to live with my aunt 600 miles away, without telling me why. I must have been shocked. I denied it all until now. Just in the last few months I've gotten in touch with my feelings that not only did that SOB abandon me, but my mother rejected me. That must have really hurt that little boy inside of me. I'm just now beginning to get angry about that, too." At a subsequent session, he told us, "One way I learned to handle people abandoning me was not to get too close to them. And with certain women, I'd get very close to them, but if any conflict came up for very long, I'd leave them right away. I can view it now that I was abandoning them before they could leave me." John continues to work on his feelings of hurt and anger in dealing with this important issue in his recovery that of abandonment.

We may have felt alone for a long time, with no one to be real with and rely on to be safe and be real back with us. Important people may have abandoned us when we were still too young and vulnerable. Or our parents may have been physically present, but emotionally absent.

With this core issue there is often low self-esteem. I may feel happier, more confident and real when someone else is there to prop me up and protect me from my fears and urges. If I'm alone, I won't be able to cope with my emotions that come up, or with my other challenges. I may believe that it is too hard to be me and that I don't have the supports and resources to make it in this hard world.

How It Shows Up

Fear of abandonment as a core issue can manifest in many ways:

• Being overly possessive or clingy,

• Intruding inappropriately into anothers' life or space,

• Being manipulative or controlling,

Wisdom to Know The Difference

- Seeking intimacy too fast with others, and

- Having frequent age regressions, abreactions, or temper tantrums.

Some examples of unresolved abandonment fears:

- a spouse accuses their mate of having an affair without any objective evidence,

- a mother forbids her teenager from being in a romantic or close relationship,

- "walking on eggshells," a mate tolerates repeated abuse in a toxic relationship,

- a boy or girlfriend calls or texts several times daily,

- your friend appears at an office event where she was not invited, and

- a divorcee stalks his ex-wife after their relationship ended.

For various reasons, all fear that they will be left alone.

A person who fears abandonment may have an attitude that "I must never do anything to bother or upset important people in my life. I have to keep them happy to keep me safe." Some leave relationships to avoid rejection. Then they may immediately start reaching out for a new someone or anyone to fill their emptiness.

If I am afraid that you or others will abandon me, then a number of problems will likely develop for me and for our relationship. Having a substantial fear of abandonment will usually result in my inability to be real and be my True Self with you and to set and maintain healthy boundaries. Since my True Self is the only part of me that can know and set healthy boundaries, and since healthy boundaries protect and maintain the integrity and well-being of my True Self, these two —actor and action, being and boundary —work together to begin healing each of my core issues.

INTERACTIONS WITH OTHER CORE ISSUES

We need, often want and sometimes crave authentic relationship. Relationships may cover a spectrum from being *casual* to *close* to *intimate*. If I am insecure within myself, if I do not know and live from and as my True Self, then the *threat of the other's abandoning me* may prevent me from ever beginning to set healthy boundaries. Living then from a false self, often with unhealthy boundaries, a number of other core issues may be set into motion and then may become aggravated, including as in the following example diagram. Figure 7.1 shows how fear of abandonment can interact with the other core issues and ultimately block our ability to be real.

Figure 7.1 **Inter-relationships among Core Recovery Issues:**
From the perspective of **fear of abandonment,**
which ultimately may block **ability to be Real.**

These other core issues influence and interact with fear of abandonment in many ways. I show some examples in Table 7.1.

To heal from disabling abandonment fears we can work a full recovery program as I describe on page 4 above and in my other books. This includes working through our other core issues, and especially difficulty trusting and shame. Psychologist Simon Hearn writes that healing abandonment fear is also based on the idea that inside of us there is a competent, self-supporting person who wants to come out.

TABLE 7.1. INTERACTIONS AMONG FEAR OF ABANDONMENT WITH OTHER CORE ISSUES

Core Issues	Influence and Interactions
Needing to be in Control	If I control you just enough you won't leave me
High tolerance for inappropriate behavior	If I tolerate your inappropriate behavior, you may not leave me
All-or-None	If you stay with me, I live. If you leave me, I die
Being Real	Fear of abandonment often prevents our being real
Trust	To counter our fear of abandonment we often mistrust
Feelings	We shut out our feelings so we don't feel the fear & hurt
Shame	With this issue there is often a low self-esteem

Of course, that is our Real Self fully realized. The goal is not to be coldly self-sufficient or never needing others. The aim is to be your own person and move from *needing* relationships (to avoid being alone) to *wanting* and *enjoying* relationships.

8 HIGH TOLERANCE FOR INAPPROPRIATE BEHAVIOR

As adult children from troubled or dysfunctional families, we may have grown up not knowing what was "normal," healthy or appropriate behavior from others. Having no other reference point from which to test reality, we may think that these behaviors and our experience with our family and our life, with its inconsistency, its trauma and pain, are "the way it is." In fact, when we live as our false self, which troubled families, relationships and work environments tend to promote, we become fixed in this role—and we don't realize that there is any other way to be.

With appropriate supervision and feedback from skilled and safe others (therapists, sponsors and peers in recovery and other relationships), we slowly learn what is healthy and appropriate. Other closely related core issues include: being overly-responsible for others, neglecting our own needs, difficulty handling feelings, boundary issues and shame.

Tim was a 30-year-old single man who had been in our therapy group for two months. He told us, "When I was a kid, I felt trapped into having to listen to my father's loud, irrational talk and behavior when he was drinking, which was most every night and weekends. When I tried to get away from him, I felt so guilty. My mother added to it by telling me how selfish I was. Even today as an adult, I let people treat me badly. I let some almost walk all over me. But until I found out about recovery and started reading about it and going to meetings, I thought something was wrong with me." Tim is learning about his high tolerance of others' inappropriate behavior and is beginning to get free of this often subtle effect of mistreatment.

WHAT IS INAPPROPRIATE BEHAVIOR?

On the surface, "inappropriate" means not suitable or proper for either an individual or a general circumstance. Inappropriate *behavior* (IB) can happen over a spectrum of various personal and group actions that are usually recognized as unpleasant, hurtful or painful in some way to the observer and sometimes to the one doing the IB. We can experience these as a child, teen or adult. Most IB enactors exhibit some of the characteristics of unsafe people, as discussed on page 47. I summarize common examples of IB in Table 8.1 on the next page.

TABLE 8.1 INAPPROPRIATE BEHAVIORS (as Hurts, Losses and Traumas)

from *Family of Origin, in School or elsewhere* (experienced as a child or teen)	from *Adult or Current Experience* (experienced as an adult)
Psychological Abuse - Tease,* threaten, bully, judge, compare unfairly, blame, shame, guilt, invalidate, "take your inventory," break a significant promise; ... yell or scream any of these. Role reversal, use, exploit (narcissistic parent); invalidate feelings & experience	
Physical Abuse – Hit, slap, push, kick, bruise, burn, scratch, choke	Same, as physical or domestic violence
Sexual abuse *Covert* – Sexual jokes, inappropriate nudity, sexual preoccupation *Overt* – Sexual touch, stimulation, penetration, threats	Sexual, gender, religious harassment or the like Rape, inappropriate touching
Neglect – Little or no: attention, love, guidance, fathering or mothering, healthy modeling; Food, shelter, clothes, education, medical care	Varies for situation

* Indicates unfair, vicious or toxic teasing (see Appendix A.5. on page 275)

What are **not** Inappropriate Behaviors (Hurts, Losses and Traumas) for a *Child*: *Appropriate boundaries and limits*.

For both *child* and *adult*: Different preferences, decisions, simple disagreements, ordinary conflicts; transferences, mistakes and the like.

WHO DOES IT?

Who can exhibit or show inappropriate behavior? How can we recognize them? They can be anyone, from individuals to groups, from members of our family-of-origin to outside relationships to co-workers to strangers to authority figures, governments and others, as shown in Table 8.2 below.

These people may not maliciously or purposefully enact or exhibit inappropriate behavior. Instead, they may be acting out effects of their own traumas and/or be actively alcohol or other drug dependent—including to toxic psychiatric drugs. Some perpetrators may have a personality disorder or worse, at the extreme, as psychiatrist Scott Peck described in his 1983 book *People of the Lie*. [76]

Some of the above enactors—many of whom are not in recovery, self-actualized or healthy enough to be safe people for us—will from sometimes-to-often unknowingly or even knowingly exhibit inappropriate behavior. At times the inappropriate behavior is abuse, trauma or neglect. Inappropriate behavior may be hurtful to us, to the enactor or to others.

TABLE 8.2. POTENTIAL PEOPLE WHO MAY ENACT INAPPROPRIATE BEHAVIOR

Individual People	Groups of People
Family - parents, siblings, other relatives	
Relationships - friends & acquaintances, close friends, spouse	**Politicians, lawmakers** - county, state, federal *
Co-workers - peers, bosses, supervisors	**Law enforcement** - police, judges, agencies
Others - teachers, religious leaders, peers, clinicians, strangers	**Other** authority figures & groups

* *He who chooses security over freedom will have neither*.   —Ben Franklin

If it is not hurtful to us, it is usually *none of our business*—unless we see someone harming a child to whom we may be close.

HOW IT DEVELOPS

High tolerance for inappropriate behavior usually develops over time from repeated childhood and later traumas that stifle our Real Self and block our healthy God-given freedoms and healthy relationship skills, coping mechanisms and other useful conditions. In Table 8.3 I *contrast* these healthy and appropriate characteristics and experiences *learned in healthy* families, people, groups and societies with those that are *unhealthy* and *traumatic*. High tolerance for inappropriate behavior usually results from and is then intricately interwoven with having experienced repeated trauma. These traumas and other effects of repeated traumas keep the victim frozen and subservient, with frequent age regressions, often isolated and captive to the inappropriate behavior of their abusers.

John and Linda Friel said that the genesis of high tolerance for inappropriate behavior has several origins that show how as children we become saints and martyrs and then as adults we try to remain so. It comes from: 1) learning to deny our feelings when we are little, often to protect ourselves from abuse; 2) seeing one or both of our parents repeatedly refuse to take care of their own healthy human needs; 3) religious or cultural rules that say others must always come first; 4) watching self-destructive patterns of living in our parents who work, drink, take care of others, yell, lie and even play too much. Through years of putting others first and our own self-denial, we come to pride ourselves in just how much pain we can put up with before we say "Ouch!" [38]

TABLE 8.3 HEALTHY V. UNHEALTHY RELATIONSHIP SKILLS & CONDITIONS TO HANDLE HIGH TOLERANCE FOR INAPPROPRIATE BEHAVIOR

Healthy family/relationship conditions & skills	Unhealthy conditions from family & other groups
Freedom to be real	Others stifle our freedom
Freedom to realize Individuation and independence	Fusion, enmeshment, unhealthy dependence
Privacy	Invasion, intrusion
Healthy boundaries	Loose boundaries
Healthy 2-way relationships	Triangles
Self actualization	Lost selfhood, codependence
Free speech	No talk rule, political correctness
Keep what is ours and what we earn	Conscription of our possessions/earnings

Examples: "Doesn't it bother you that your mother is always so critical of you?" a healthy friend asks. "Well no," you say with hesitation, "She had such a hard life. I understand why she does it." "It's fine that you understand why she does it. But is it healthy for you to subject yourself to such abuse, day in and day out?" What does that do to a person over the years? It's simple. It teaches us to discount and abuse ourselves.

The Friels continue, "As adults who have learned to tolerate lots of inappropriate behavior from others, we find ourselves replaying our childhoods in our current relationships where our partners lie to us repeatedly, or hurt us physically, or criticize us unmercifully, and we just stay with that person. We make lots of excuses for their behavior. We pride ourselves in how tolerant and patient we are. We begin to believe that we are better than everyone else, because the only people we let into our lives are abusive people. The popular saying 'Life's a ***** and Then You Die' becomes our credo. We pray a lot, but we don't do anything to get out of the destructive relationship. We try to reform for the other person, always hoping that today will be the day that she or he will change. But change rarely happens by itself."

"What would someone with a full cup do when faced with an abusive or manipulative relationship? Our nine year old son said it best. We took him and our two daughters to see the film version of 'The Color Purple' when it was first released. As we discussed the film in the kitchen that evening, David stood silent for a moment, and then thoughtfully asked, 'Why didn't she just leave?' That, of course, is what someone with a full cup would do. They'd simply leave." [38]

FURTHER MANIFESTATIONS, DYNAMICS AND RECOVERY AIDS

High-stress families and others often increase our tolerance for unsafe or negative situations by teaching us inappropriate "standards" of acceptable behavior. As a result of this "high tolerance" we accept abuses, often because we experienced similar situations in and outside of our home. For example, if a parent was an alcoholic, drinking a beer for breakfast may seem "normal" to us. If we have developed a high tolerance, we may begin to think all relationships involve screaming, jealousy, domestic violence, or other abusive behaviors. Our high tolerance assures us that those painful situations will continue in our life.

To reduce problems created by a high tolerance for these dysfunctional situations, it may be helpful to seek out the experience and opinion of someone you consider emotionally and socially healthy. Likely places to find such people are in Twelve Step groups, group therapy, individual therapy, and with healthy friends. If we want healthy relationships, we seek guidance from people who themselves already have healthy relationships. If we want a stable, calm life–seek *association with* and *guidance* from those who have a *stable* and *calm* life. We transform high tolerance for inappropriate behavior into knowing what is appropriate by asking a safe person. We use our observation of another's inappropriate behavior by recognizing that we are being mistreated. And if so, setting healthy boundaries and limits and preventing further mistreatment.

Psychologist Joseph Carver said, "After a series of abusive or poor relationships–a new healthy one might actually seem uncomfortable or strange. [15] If we have a temper tantrum and tell the healthy individual 'Get out of my life' – that's what they may do. They may not yell and scream, fight back, or try to fix the situation. They may not throw a brick through your window with an 'I Love You' note tied to it. Their healthy decision is to avoid a relationship that includes aggressiveness, tantrums, or other forms of high-stress drama. After an abusive relationship, we may feel our healthy [new] partner doesn't love us because they aren't aggressively or violently jealous. We use our background and experiences to evaluate and judge our current situations. ...We may unintentionally avoid healthy partners because they don't act like our past abusive, controlling or emotionally-detached partners."

Psychiatrist Richard Kluft describes eight closely-related symptom clusters that trauma survivors commonly experience and show (Table 8.4). While he originally wrote these symptom groups to apply to survivors of child sexual abuse known as incest, in others' and my experience most of them also apply to survivors of other kinds of repeated childhood trauma. The latter two of these symptom clusters (see **bolded**) describe some of the most common of the many manifestations of people who often experience high tolerance for inappropriate behavior and a closely related relationship style often called co-dependence.

Virginia Satir suggested that half of people commonly respond as a "people pleaser," appeaser or placater. They say yes to others regardless of what they actually prefer, want or feel in a situation. They take all responsibility onto themselves. They over-respect others' views, but not their own. This stance may draw sympathy, but can appear weak. They will use distortion, all-or-none thinking and other defenses-against-pain to shift blame to themselves. They typically have open body language with palms up, or out towards the audience or other person and hunched shoulders.

TABLE 8.4 SYMPTOM CLUSTERS IN VICTIMS OF INCEST: NOTE THAT ALL THESE EFFECTS MIMIC "MENTAL ILLNESS" FROM KLUFT 2010

Symptom cluster	Description
Emotional incontinence	An inability to contain distressing effects and the urges that accompany them
Affective dysregulation	The intrusion of strong emotions and/or their suppression
Dysfunctional self-soothing	Use of addictive substances, activities, rituals of self-harm or self-stimulation
Somatoform dissociation	Physical expressions of emotional distress
Co-morbidity	The effects of trauma-related conditions, physical and mental
Sexual dysfunction	Inhibitions, dyscontrol, and reenactment-driven compulsive sexuality
Reenacting & re-victimization behaviors	Efforts to **please, charm, withdraw, defy, place self at risk for further trauma**, etc
Failures in relatedness (Kluft: Psychiatric Times. Vol. 27 No. 12, 2011)	Efforts to play a role that is **pleasing or not offensive to others, while mistrusting/over-trusting others; often experience neither intimacy, nurture, or support, but continue involved with them**

As children they learn early to overlook or smooth over potentially upsetting family situations. They may try to sense what others are feeling, at the expense of their own feelings. They tend to have a high tolerance for inappropriate behavior. Many become helping professionals, which can reinforce their tendencies to ignore their own needs. Others can get annoyed when we are so passive or indecisive. Or they can blame us and try to dominate or take control.

Placaters can sacrifice themselves for others and will lose so others can win. "Whatever you want, don't worry about me, I'm nothing." They come across as victims. They play "softball" in negotiations. We think of this as a weak position, but there are times when it can be a useful strategy. For instance when playing with small children, when diplomacy is needed (How do you treat a cop who stops you?) or to give the *appearance* of weakness.

UNHEALTHY BOUNDARIES LEAD
TO HIGH TOLERANCE

To keep you from leaving me (fear of abandonment), I may loosen my boundaries to such an extent that you can mistreat me. I will repeatedly allow you to mistreat me or others, in hopes that you won't leave me. With an already low self-esteem, I may not realize that I don't deserve to be treated this way. I don't deserve your hurtful, inappropriate behavior. Since I don't yet fully know my True Self and since I have unhealthy boundaries, I may let you invade my personal space inordinately. Is there any limit to how badly and how often I will let you mistreat me? Figure 8.1 shows some key dynamics in this core issue about how other factors and issues interact with it.

At times someone's behavior may only *remind* me of what *another* did to me in the past (a transference or a projection), but it is not actually inappropriate behavior (if in doubt check that out with a safe friend or clinician).

HEALING FROM HIGH TOLERANCE FOR INAPPROPRIATE BEHAVIOR

High tolerance for inappropriate behavior is a defense that we may have learned to help us survive a troubled or dysfunctional family and/or another abusive group. We can also learn that using it repeatedly makes us more vulnerable to further abuse and neglect. But in recovery we can learn that —to survive and later even thrive— continuing our high tolerance defense against emotional pain is no longer necessary.

To get free from other people's inappropriate behavior usually requires establishing and maintaining healthy boundaries and limits. To be able to set these boundaries we have to find and be our Real Self. To do that we can follow the actions and principles below.

Figure 8.1 Dynamics in High Tolerance for Inappropriate Behavior

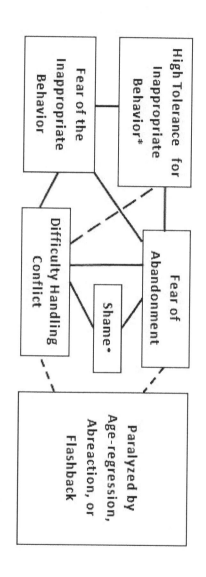

* Low self-esteem (shame) is commonly involved and underlies most of these dynamics. There may also be a "pseudo inappropriate behavior" involved at times, i.e., it only *reminds* me of what another did to me in the past (a transference or a projection), but it is not actually inappropriate behavior (check it out with a safe friend or clinician if in doubt).

HEALING HIGH TOLERANCE
FOR INAPPROPRIATE BEHAVIOR

- Begin a Stage 2 full recovery program

  (see Table A.4 on page 273 of the Appendix)

- Name the core issue(s) as they occur

- Name the inappropriate behavior

- Set boundaries and limits as fitting

- Grieve the past inappropriate behaviors (traumas)

- Learn to tolerate emotional pain

  ...Who does all this? Our Real Self

  ...Which helps by letting go of
  false self (ego)

  ...With help from God/ Higher Power
  (when we ask)

  "Let go, Let God" Twelve Step saying

  *   *   *

In the next chapter I will address a core issue that commonly occurs with high tolerance for inappropriate behavior: difficulty handling conflict.

9   DIFFICULTY HANDLING CONFLICT

Difficulty handling and resolving conflict is a common core issue in all three recovery stages. It usually interacts with most of the other core issues. Growing up in a troubled or dysfunctional family, to survive the pain we learn to avoid conflict whenever we can. We may have seen our parents and other family members model poor conflict handling and resolution. When conflict occurs, we learn to withdraw from it in some way. Occasionally, we become aggressive, and try to overpower and control those with whom we are in conflict. When these actions fail, we may become devious and attempt to manipulate. In a dysfunctional environment, using these methods may help assure our survival. But they do not tend to work for us in a healthy intimate relationship.

Recovery begins by observing each conflict as it comes up and then working through it. But the fear and other painful feelings that come up as we get closer to the conflict may be too much for us to experience. Rather than face the pain and the conflict head-on, we may revert to our prior methods of all-or-none and the like by over-controlling or withdrawing.

Joanne was a 40-year-old woman who had been in group therapy for adult children of dysfunctional families for seven months. She tried to be the dominant member of the group. But when Ken joined the group, he tried to be assertive with her, and at times was aggressive enough to cause her difficulty and frustration in being as dominant as she had been. After several altercations between Joanne and Ken, Joanne announced that she had decided to leave the group. Upon exploration by the group, their basic conflict was revealed. My co-leader and I said, "Joanne, Ken, and the group are at a crucial point in their recovery. You are right in the middle of an important conflict. You have an opportunity here, since this group is a safe place, to work through a core issue for each of you. In the past how have you handled conflict?"

The group members discussed how they often ran away from it, or became aggressive or even manipulative, and that had not worked for them. Another group member said to Joanne, "You really do have a chance to work this thing through. I hope you don't leave." She said she would think about it, and the next week she returned and said she had decided to stay in the group.

She told the group that she felt that they didn't listen to her and support her, and that since Ken had joined the group, she had felt that more so. More issues were revealed, including that she had always had difficulty recognizing her needs and getting them met. She also had always felt unappreciated, misunderstood, unheard, unsupported and unloved by her parents. She, Ken, and the group worked on their conflict, and over the course of several group therapy sessions, resolved it.

In handling and resolving conflict we first *recognize* that we *are in it*. We *name* the issue as that we are *in conflict* and that we may need to go within and with safe others and *explore how* to resolve it. We then take a risk if we feel safe, to disclose our concerns, feelings, wants and needs. It is nearly always useful not to scream or yell at the other(s) with whom we may be in conflict, since doing so usually escalates and elevates the conflict to un-resolvable levels. By working through conflict, we gradually learn to identify and work through our past conflicts and current ones as they come up for us. It takes courage to recognize and to work through conflict.

DEFINING CONFLICT

When we make a decision or take an action that is OK with us and those around us, there is usually no resulting conflict. It becomes a conflict only when others disagree and we get upset with that. A conflict is usually a *disagreement* between two or more people when they perceive a *threat* to their wants, needs, interests or concerns. The possible threats span a spectrum from the mundane (common) to life threatening (rare). Although occasional conflict is normal and usually gives us a *chance for growth* through improved understanding, insight and skills, some see it as a negative experience. At first we may see limited options and resources for solutions, rather than the multiple possibilities that may exist "outside the box" in which we are problem-solving.

Of course the *true* threat versus our *perceived* disagreement and threat may be different. Conflicts tend to have levels of misunderstanding that can exaggerate these basic conflict areas. Understanding the true aspects of a disagreement can help us solve both parties' problems. We work to identify and understand the true threat (issues) and develop strategies and solutions to resolve it.

We may filter our perceptions and reactions through our experience, beliefs, information, wants, needs, values, culture, gender, and the like. Our responses are often filled with ideas and feelings that can be strong and powerful guides to our possible solutions. Using creative problem-solving strategies help us reach positive results. We may need to re-think and reframe our conflict from one in which it is "my way or the highway" (all-or-none) into one in which we entertain new possibilities that have been otherwise elusive.

WE ARE THE HERO

In his classic book *The Hero with a Thousand Faces*, the master teacher and mythologist Joseph Campbell described the hero's journey. The ancient Greek literature described conflict as the *agon* or *central contest*. Aristotle said that in order to hold our interest, the hero must have a single conflict. This *act* of the conflict involves the protagonist (the hero/heroine or "first fighter") and the antagonist (the villain whom our hero fights). For the hero story, ideally the outcome of the contest cannot usually be known in advance, and the hero's struggle should be ennobling. In our recovery and our life as we struggle in each of our conflicts, *we* are *each* the hero/heroine. [17,18,75] I summarize and illustrate that in *Healing the Child Within* and simplify it here with references to the A.A. and other

Twelve Step fellowships in Figure 9.1. I will say more about this dynamic in the next chapter.

Figure 9.1 The Mythical Hero-Heroine's Journey*

* from Jos. Campbell & AA literature

KINDS OF CONFLICT

There are 7 main *adversaries* in conflict: Person vs: 1) *Self* (internal conflict), vs. 2) *Another Person*, 3) *Society/world*, 4) *Nature*, 5) *Technology*, 6) *God*, and 7) *"Fate."*

Professional mediators divide Person v *person* conflicts into at least 7 *types*: those involving *relationship*, *information* / data, *interest*, *structure*, *past history*, *psychological* aspects and *value*. Most conflicts will have one or more of these elements as root causes. Generally, a solution to a conflict will match its type or cause. Many conflicts will involve a *combination* of two or more of these. By evaluating a conflict according to these areas we can begin to determine the causes of a conflict and plan ways to resolve it. I describe these conflict types *generally* and conflicts in the *workplace* further in section A.2 on page 286 in the Appendix.

FACTORS THAT TRIGGER CONFLICTS AND BLOCK RESOLUTION

Over the decades assisting countless trauma survivors and researching the clinical aspects of trauma, I have identified 9 common factors or situations that trigger conflicts *and* block their healing and resolution (Figure 9.2). A conflict often develops when we don't get something important that we want in our life or when we get something that we *don't* want. When *in addition* any one or more of these 9 factors shown are present, they often prompt an even stronger reaction that we are in a conflict—but we often feel as though we are unable to resolve it. Going clock-wise around this figure, to explain or review the role of *age regression*, consider reading or re-reading parts of Chapter 6 above. For information on how *psychiatric drugs* trigger us to be in a conflict—or feeling as though we are in one—consider reading the sections on drug toxicity in psychiatrist Peter Breggin's books or in my book *Not Crazy: You May Not Be Mentally Ill.*[9,103] *Negative imagination* is the opposite of creative, constructive, productive imagination. It spans a spectrum from needless worry or ruminating to Catastrophizing, which may also be associated with any of the 8 other factors. Negative imagination can also appear as any of the guises of all-or-none thinking as outlined in Table 4.1 on page 32.

If we get close to anyone with a *personality disorder*, their frequent inappropriate behavior can often trigger repeated conflicts for us. If we remain close to them, most people with a personality disorder will be toxic to our well-being, and if we cater to their or others' crazy demands we may find that we are *co-dependent* (focusing on them or others to our detriment). We may get involved in other *toxic relationships* that can also trigger us to feel much distress. We may get involved with someone with an *active addiction*, which can eventually look and feel for us as though we are losing our mind. We ourself may have an active addiction that generates dysfunctional and disruptive effects that trigger repeated conflicts for us and for others close to us. We may have perhaps the most common cause of conflicts: *ego attachment*, whereby we let our ego/false self take over our life and which makes more negative imagination against us. We and/or another in our life may also have *active PTSD* that disrupts many aspects of our life, including interacting with several of the other triggering factors shown in Figure 9.2.

Finally, all of these factors often *block* our ability to solve and resolve any conflict that they may have generated. Until the factor/factors is/are addressed, difficulty handling conflict will likely continue to be a common problem for us. In the psychological area within conflicts there may be a desire for power, control, autonomy, attention, recognition or love—most of which may involve other core issues. There are times when these basic human tendencies and drives will be contributing to a conflict, often masquerading as some other, deeper or more causal issue. Few people are going to be able to say "I'm in this conflict with you because you're not giving me enough attention or recognition." To resolve the conflict it sometimes could be wisest not to deal with these more base issues directly. If we become aware of these dynamics, it may be useful to search for a viable solution so that some of these needs will be met, and will thereby reduce the need to create more conflict (basic "Conflict 101").

*   *   *

Because difficulty handling conflict is such a common problem, I will cover several positive ways to handle it in the next chapter.

FIGURE 9.2. 9 FACTORS TRIGGER & AGGRAVATE CONFLICTS AMONG TRAUMA SURVIVORS & BLOCK HEALING & RESOLUTION

10   DIFFICULTY HANDLING CONFLICT - PART 2

CHOICES IN HANDLING CONFLICTS

Before recovery, many of us may have used an all-or-none approach to handle our conflicts. We fight or attack the other party. Or we may run away, withdraw, hide or decline to engage them in working through our differences. While some minor conflicts may for the most part be appropriately and successfully ignored (see lower 2 rows of Table 10.1), the most efficient approach is usually to face it head-on, engage the other party as needed and work it through (Table 10.2).

Depending on who we may be in conflict with, we usually have several choices regarding which problem solving tools or skills we can enlist. For a general or generic approach to resolve a conflict, consider using a problem-solving approach as I outline in Table 10.3 below. First, determine the 3 most important details of your conflict and write them underneath the *Problem(s)* heading.

TABLE 10.1 LEVELS, CONSEQUENCES AND ATTENTION NEEDED TO HELP SOLVE CONFLICTS (see text section Threat, Attention and Time in Conflicts 4 pages below for more details)

Level	Threats & Consequences	Attention*	Possible Lessons Learned
5	Life threatening	Total focus required	• Sort out or prioritize each conflict's seriousness.
4	**Major** loss *probable*	Near total focus	
3	Major loss *possible*, but unlikely	More as needed to prevent the loss	• If a low threat, identify & address any of the 9 triggering factors in Fig. 9.2.
2	**Minor** loss *probable*	Some as needed	• Use a combined mental & spiritual approach to resolve conflict.
1	Minor loss *possible*, but unlikely	Little	• Remember & repeat the Serenity Prayer when need.
0	Inconsequential	Little or none	

* For all conflict levels, gathering **more information** usually helps resolve it, as described on page 114 below.

Then do the same for each of the other headings, and now you will have a plan for resolving your conflict. How much focus you devote to your plan and how much action you take will determine how likely you will be to resolve your conflict. For committed couples who may often fight unfairly (yelling, screaming, threatening, "taking our inventory,"

TABLE 10.2. POSSIBLE METHODS AND SOLUTIONS TO HANDLING CONFLICTS

Possible Solutions	Description & Comments
1. **Fight**	Attack the other party verbally
2. **Flight (Run away)**	Withdraw, hide, decline engaging in working it through.
3. **Engage the conflict & work it through**	Usually the most productive. Can use a general approach or consider 4 other ways as shown below.
• **Fair Fighting**	Developed for couples who tend to fight unfairly (page 293).
• **Approach by Spiritual Levels (with Humility)**	Understanding the usual conflict in triangles, this allows new and higher ways to solve many conflicts. See p 289 in Appendix
• **ego detachment**	As described in from AA/Al-Anon to *A Course in Miracles*
• **Admit powerless over** _____	As in Step One of the Twelve Steps; use Serenity Prayer

shaming, or using the "silent treatment") we can use a structured but effective method called *fair fighting*, as summarized in Section A.4 on page 293 in the Appendix. For anyone, including committed couples, relatives, business partners, or the like wherein the two parties-in-conflict have already triangled-in a third party (such as a child, friend, relative, employee, co-worker, or the like) using a *healthy boundaries* and *spiritual levels-oriented approach* with humility can often help us solve the conflict (summarized in Section A.3 on page 289 in the Appendix).

TABLE 10.3. GENERAL OR GENERIC APPROACH TO PLAN RESOLVING A CONFLICT

Problem(s) Main details of the conflict	Objectives/ Goals What you want to happen	Methods/ Actions How to get what you want	Evaluation How to know you got it
Fill in the 3 most important ...	...for each heading		

INTERNAL CONFLICT

Although most of our conflicts may appear to involve one or more outside parties, in fact most also involve our inner life (page 5). Most conflicts have varying degrees of inner life involvement, especially for those with higher threat and consequence, as listed in Table 10.1 above. This inner life activation tends to stir up both emotional pain *and* a reaction to try to lessen our pain and hopefully resolve both pain and conflict.

This internal conflict tends to show up for us through a number of dynamics, manifestations and experiences, which I summarize in Table 10.4. When we find ourself in a conflict,

TABLE 10.4. COMMON DYNAMICS AND MANIFESTATIONS OF INTERNAL CONFLICT (PERSON V. SELF) *SUMMARIZED*

Type	Description/Comment
Age Regression	Sudden paralysis of our psyche/mind/feelings (see page 52)
Abreaction	A dramatic age regression acted out or in
Re-enactment	Unconscious repeating of a painful action or experience from our past to try to heal it
Mis-perception	Seeing, hearing or interpreting things wrongly or incorrectly
ego defenses	Unconscious ego-mind trick to protect us from emotional pain; see Appendix
Projection	Unconscious ascription of a personal thought, feeling, or impulse, esp. if considered undesirable, onto somebody else; an ego defense
Addiction	Unhealthy attachment to people, places or things that may lessen our emotional pain temporarily
Core issues	Unconscious dynamics that protect us from emotional pain; see page 13

we can first identify and name that we are in a conflict and then go within to search for which of these inner life dynamics we may be experiencing. To help us resolve the conflict we then name the issue or dynamic and express our experience with it to a safe person or group (such as a therapy group or a Twelve Step Group). Of course, a major cause of conflict and a block to their resolution is ego *attachment* and *inflation*, which I address below.

THREAT, ATTENTION AND TIME IN CONFLICTS

In a conflict, how serious will it be if you do not get what you want? How much time and attention should you devote to it? The least that a conflict's *threat* and *consequence* may be, the less attention and time that we usually need to devote to it, as shown in Table 10.1 above. But for excessive worriers, drama queens and kings and some with "OCD," they may spend more time focused on their minor conflicts than they need. They may even waste their time worrying about them unnecessarily. Spending too much time can ultimately add to their difficulty handling the conflict. In these cases it can be useful to remember and repeat the Serenity Prayer (see Chapter 1).

In my clinical experience, many to most excessive worriers—when a careful trauma history is taken—will have PTSD. "Depression," "anxiety disorder," and "OCD" are all usually surface labels that often contribute little or nothing to the person's insight, understanding and recovery potential and reality. When they realize that they have PTSD instead, which is a normal reaction to serious or repeated trauma, they have a far better chance to begin recovery and eventually experience peace. When a conflict comes up for us we can now consider how serious its consequences may be, and based on that, how much attention we may need to give it. With our new extra time, we can now, instead, consider whether any of the 9 factors may be contributing to our repeated conflicts or whether they are blocking their resolution (Figure 9.2 in the previous chapter).

EGO DETACHMENT

Another effective way to handle and resolve a conflict is to recognize when we are in our ego and then detach from it. *A Course in Miracles* is a modern spiritual text that millions have read and studied. The Course says that we know when we are *in our ego* when we are *not at peace*. The Course is the most spiritually informative and exciting book I have ever read. I have found no other spiritual writing as intellectually stimulating, yet so practical in our relationships with self, others and God. Do you want to feel peace or pain? If you want peace, the Course suggests, choose God. It's that simple. What is not so simple is knowing exactly why, when and how to choose God. The Course addresses conflict directly or indirectly on nearly every page. [101, 102]

The Course says that a miracle is a *shift in perception* that happens when we *choose God* or God's Holy Spirit *over the ego*. This choosing then brings about a psychological and spiritual *correction* in our *thinking*, *feeling* or *behaving* that otherwise may be causing us *conflict* and *pain*. In this sense, the miracle is the *healing* of our conflict and pain. The Course says that the part of our psyche that chooses God—or not—is our *mind*. When our mind *chooses* God, the Holy Spirit and/or Christ, the Course calls it *right* mind, which is perhaps the closest term to the True or Real Self, or Child Within, that it uses. When it chooses the ego (or false self), it calls it *wrong* mind. The main way that we choose God is through simple prayer. The easiest effective prayer is "Help"—when we are sincere and surrender to let go and let God help us. [101, 102]

I have noticed that when I am in conflict and feel pain from it, that I can usually bring about a miracle. I pause, ask God (or Holy Spirit or Christ) for help, and within a few seconds or a few minutes I usually feel less pain and more peace. For me, that process and experience are what I understand to be a miracle. Sometimes that one miracle experience is enough to help my particular conflict. At other times I will need to ask for help again, and sometimes ask several more times. But what is important to me is that my asking usually works. I've also noticed that once I've prayed, within a short or longer time something intervenes in my life that is more gentle, creative, and powerful in a healing way than anything I would have imagined. This choice for God and the ensuing experience of peace is gratifying.

The Course's message is similar to the Twelve Step programs of AA, Al-Anon and other fellowships that throughout their literature talk of ego detachment—embodied and summarized in their simple statement "Let go and let God." There are several such references to *ego*, *being egocentric*, and *selfishness* as being "the root of our troubles," and that these are "Driven by a hundred forms of fear, self delusion, self-seeking and self-pity." (AA "Big Book" p 62; and *As Bill Sees It*). [3b, 5]

TELLING OUR STORY

Part of resolving conflict and healing conflicts of all sorts is by telling our story authentically from our real self to safe and supportive people. This can be with a safe friend (see page 48), an individual therapist or counselor, or a group such as a therapy group or a Twelve Step fellowship group. When we tell our story, we can follow the tried-and-true Twelve Step fellowship group structure of: 1) What we were like, 2) What happened, and 3) What we're like now. Most first-timers may not know about this potential structural advantage, so the therapist will have to guide them and the safe friend will *listen patiently* without trying to give advice or change them. But the safe friend can give them empathy, compassion and support as they work through their issues. Telling our story involves all of the other models in Table 10.5 and the various dimensions of Figure 9.1 on the Hero's journey above. To make these possibilities work we can simply try them. To prepare, we can write them out in a journal or use the outline above in Table 10.3 to address working through any conflict. For more on telling our story see chapter 16.

ADDICTIONS AND PTSD CAN CAUSE AND AGGRAVATE CONFLICTS

Distractions of all sorts commonly interfere with our ability to handle conflict. Active addictions and PTSD not only commonly distract us from handling conflicts well, but they often *cause* and *aggravate* these conflicts in our life.

As I wrote in my book *Not Crazy*: You May Not be Mentally Ill, active addictions can generate any or all of the spectrum of symptoms of mental illness, from anxiety to "depression" to dysfunctional behaviors to psychosis (Table 6.1 above), most of which can lead to causing and aggravating conflicts.

TABLE 10.5. PHASES OF OUR LIFE JOURNEY AND OUR STORIES ACCORDING TO 6 MODELS OR VIEWS

Model or View	Phases of our Life Journey and our Stories		
	1	2	3
Telling our story	What we were like	What happened	What we're like now
Disease model	Genesis (pathogenesis)	Active illness	Healing and recovery
Classical mythology	Separation	Initiation	Return / rebirth
Levels of consciousness	Lower self/ego Unconscious	Acceptance through conflict as Real Self	Higher Self / God consciousness
Spiritual	Forgetting & separating	Suffering (resisting what is)	Remembering & letting go
Thanatological	Death	Hit "bottom"	Rebirth
Core Issues Healing	Early / Unaware / Stuck in	Awakening / Working on and through	Advanced Recovery

FIGURE 10.2. DYNAMICS & MANIFESTATIONS OF INTERNAL CONFLICT (PERSON V. SELF)

A problem is that too many people who know the symptomatic or troubled person, from clinicians to family, friends, teachers or co-workers, are *not usually aware* of these facts and associations. They commonly misdiagnose the distressed person as having one or more mental disorders and are quick to mis-prescribe or mis-recommend one or more psych *drugs*, which themselves *cause psychiatric symptoms* directly or indirectly through withdrawal and other toxic effects, as I show in Figure 10.3 on the next page. Study this figure and notice how these multiple conditions and factors come from childhood trauma and interact to cause an increased number of conflicts and difficulty causing them.

TABLE 10.6 ADDICTIONS ±PTSD CAN PRESENT AS ANY OF THE FOLLOWING —

Depression	Unstable emotions	Difficulty focusing "ADHD"	Hyper-active/ -vigilant
Low energy	Anger outbursts	Social detachment or estrangement	Flashbacks
Anxiety	Fears and phobias	Panic attacks	OCD-like symptoms
Insomnia	Nightmares	Dissociation	"Bipolar"

Having bought the claim that they have a "mental disorder," once the person begins taking a psych drug, they commonly become entranced, confused, numbed and/or spellbound by the drug effects. This dysfunctional state can become a factor in causing both more conflicts than usual and difficulty resolving them.

They may also have an associated active addiction to alcohol or another psychoactive drug that cause so many and varied psychological and physical symptoms that mimic all sorts of "mental illness." These interrelations have been known to some aware clinicians for years, and they tend not to misdiagnose these affected people with various "mental disorders." But most other clinicians are not so aware and not only misdiagnose their patients, but by prescribing or recommending psychiatric drugs, they expose them to toxic chemicals that commonly make them worse. [103]

FIGURE 10.3 THE COMPLEX WEB OF INTERACTIONS AMONG THE GREAT MASQUERADERS OF MENTAL ILLNESS

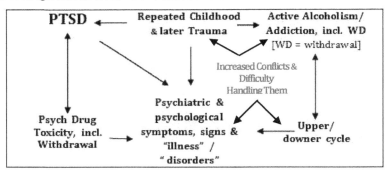

Feelings and emotions can play a big part in triggering or being in conflict and working through it. Because of this important association, in the next chapter I will address the next closely associated core issue of feelings in relationships, recovery and life.

11 FEELINGS - *INTRODUCTION*

Our feelings and emotions are usually closely involved with nearly all of the other core issues, including especially difficulty handling conflict. But just what are feelings and emotions? How are they important in our daily life? [42, 43, 53]

Silvan Tomkins and Donald Nathanson described four main kinds in this way: An **Affect** (includes our primitive feelings that last only a few seconds, such as our felt state associated with our immediate smile on seeing a loved one), [28, 72, 73, 84]

A **Feeling** (our *awareness* that an affect has been triggered, *lasting long enough* to *recognize* and *name* the specific affect),

An **Emotion** (usually lasting longer, perhaps minutes, and felt in the broader context of an experience or story), and,

A **Mood** (which is a *persisting* affect, feeling or emotion that may last from hours to days. Sometimes a mood may underlie or be in the background of the other kinds of feelings).

Imagine or picture ripples in a pond when a pebble drops from above that make concentric circles. The basic affect is inside the first small circle. A feeling is the same affect lasting longer, inside the next expanding circle. An emotion is inside the next concentric circle, and a mood is the same affect/feeling/emotion lasting still longer inside of the final circle.

Some writers lump all four of these types as simply "affect," while some call them "emotions." I refer to these generically as *feelings* throughout this chapter and this book.

There are many important questions to address about feelings as a core issue. I will address these and briefly describe the main and different kinds of feelings in this and the next chapter.

WHAT TRIGGERS THEM?

How are our feelings triggered or activated? At least six main factors may cause or trigger our feelings. These include our inner life events, outer life events, unhealthy life habits, various medical problems— including psychiatric drug toxicity (and psychiatric drug withdrawal), and perhaps what some say may be *a major cause* for painful feelings: a lack of information (Figure 11.1 and Table 11.1). I will describe some aspects of each of these now.

FIGURE 11.1 SIX MAJOR CAUSES OF PAINFUL FEELINGS

OPPOSING OBSERVATIONS

Let's begin with the first two causes or triggers in Figure 11.1 above, going clockwise, and detailed in Table 11.1 on the next page. Regarding these two triggers, there are two opposing observations: that our feelings are triggered by 1) events from the *environment* (our *outer life*) and that they are triggered by 2) our *inner life's activity*, especially our previous and current *beliefs* and *thoughts*. My sense is that they are *both true* and that they *often interact*. I outline these two views in

Table 11.2 on page 111, which shows a summary of their observed dynamics.

TABLE 11.1 MAJOR CAUSES OF PAINFUL FEELINGS *IN MORE DETAIL*

Cause or Trigger	*Possible Detailed Causes*
Inner Life Events	Trauma effects, incl. core issues such as ungrieved loss or hurt, unresolved conflict, abandonment or rejection, not getting our needs met; negative imagination, obsessive worry, other disordered thinking, lack of Information
Outer Life Events	Others abuse, neglect or hurt; physical, mental, emotional or financial injury
Unhealthy Life Habits	Junk food intake, little or no exercise, high risk behavior, nicotine, heavy alcohol or other drug use (including most psychiatric drugs) [103] See Fig 12.1
Psychiatric Drug Toxicity	Nearly all psychiatric drugs disrupt multiple brain and body systems; and their withdrawal is a common cause of emotional pain today
Medical problems	Active addictions, especially alcohol and other drug problems; PTSD, thyroid, adrenal, other endocrine illness, stroke, other disabling illness
Lack of Information	Some say this **may be** *the* **major cause** of fear, anxiety and other emotional pain (See text).

TABLE 11.2 VARIATIONS IN FEELINGS DYNAMICS & SEQUENCE WITH THOUGHTS

Trigger →	Environment: "APET" model*	Thoughts often first †
Sequence of dynamics & experiences that unfold & tend to interact with other core issues	A = Activating agent, a stimulus or trigger from the environment	Beliefs These come first many times ↓ then
	P stands for the mind's pattern-matching of the stimulus both to innate knowledge & to things learned	Thoughts These also may come first ↓
	E This, in turn gives rise to emotion.	Feelings
	T The emotion may inspire thought, although thought is not an inevitable consequence of emotional arousal.	Decisions
		Choices
		Behaviors
		Life experiences

* APET model from Griffin & Tyrell; † from Lazaris 1988

In this regard, feelings researcher and author Joe Griffin said that an emotion is simply a 'box' in which the brain initially codes incoming stimuli. "So each perception is 'tagged' in the anger box, or the anxiety box, or the sadness box. Our self-obsessed culture treats emotions as though they were something sacred and the most significant aspect of being human, rather than seeing them as a primitive classification system that usually needs further refinement. Refining perceptions is the job of the higher cortex, which can fill in the thousand shades of grey that usually exists between the black and white of emotional reasoning." Some of their reasoning can be complex, so bear with me on the next three paragraphs.

Insight into their understanding of our feelings' "pattern-matching" gave rise to what Joe Griffin and co-author Ivan Tyrell call the APET model. Our healing process centers around our eventually changing our painful ("negative") feelings to joyful ("positive") ones. When we *change* their *meaning* we "...change the template through which we experience reality." An important aspect of their model is that emotions precede thought, rather than the other way around, and that our perceptions are the meanings we attribute to certain stimuli.

In APET, the **A** stands for the **activating agent**, a **stimulus** or **trigger** from the environment. The **P** stands for the mind's

pattern-matching of the *stimulus* matching to both *innate knowledge* and to *things learned*. This, in turn gives rise to **emotion** (**E**). The emotion may inspire **thought** (**T**), although thought is not an inevitable consequence of emotional arousal. All perceptions and all thought, therefore, are "tagged" with emotion, which Griffin and Tyrrell define as "feelings that create distinctive psychobiological states, a propensity for action and simplified thinking styles. If you know that emotion precedes thought, then you know that you cannot trust yourself to act when you are emotional," Griffin said.

By contrast, Lazaris said that *beliefs* and *thoughts* usually come first, followed by feelings, then by decisions, choices, behaviors and finally life experiences. An external trigger may then enter this sequence and influence the subsequent feeling, etc. As I said above, I believe that *both* of these models operate, are true and that they *often interact*.

OTHER TRIGGERING FACTORS

Three other factors may trigger our painful feelings as shown in Figure and Table 11.1 above: *unhealthy life habits*, *psychiatric drug* toxicity and miscellaneous *medical problems*, as summarized in the table. As I describe in my book *Not Crazy* and as psychiatrist Peter Breggin details in his books, in the last 25 years psychiatric drug toxicity (including their withdrawal or missing a dose or more of them) has become an especially *common* cause of all kinds of emotional and physical pain. If you or anyone you know has a pattern of emotional upsets while taking a psych drug, the *drug may* well *be the cause*. My 2010 article "Psychiatric Drugs as Agents of Trauma" may also help here. [9, 50, 51, 70, 90, 103]

THE INFORMATION THEORY OF EMOTIONS

Some say a lack of information may be *the* major cause of fear, anxiety and other emotional pain. The Russian psychologist PV Simonov from 1964 through 1986 studied how painful feelings came about and scientifically showed that their start and continuation were so often explained by a simple formula:

$$E = N \times (NI-AI)$$

E (Emotion) = **Need** (to avoid stress) **x** (**NI** [necessary information] - **AI** [available information]). He called this the *information* theory of emotions. [80a]

A **Need** can also be seen as being a goal, want, wish, preference, drive, obsession, necessity, or a real or perceived survival factor. A need can also be wanting or needing to resolve a conflict. In getting any of these met, the more *useful* information we can find about a conflict or difficult situation that causes us emotional pain, the *less likely* will be our pain. So our task will then be to *find* and then *act on* that missing information to solve our problem and thereby decrease our pain. Sometimes at first it may not be clear which additional bit of information will prove to be useful, and so we may need to continue searching. Regarding the word *Need* in the formula, there is a difference between a real life *need* and a simpler *want* (as in "I want a new outfit to wear, although I know that I don't need it"). I describe healthy human needs in *Healing the Child Within,* reproduced in Section A.5 on page 296, and show Maslow's *Hierarchy of Needs* above on page 22.

FINDING THE INFORMATION

What *kinds* of Information might we need to have to solve a conflict, decrease our emotional pain and promote healing? Here are some kinds of missing information that we can look for:

- **New**: **Knowledge**,
- -------**Skills**
  (mental, emotional, social, spiritual),
- -------**Concept(s)**,
- **What others are thinking, feeling** and **planning**,
- **Usefulness of communication** between those in conflict,
- **What** will **likely happen**,

- **What's best for me** to do **next**,
- How to **recognize**, **name** and **handle** any *core issues* as they appear.

Also consider using trial and error if any doubt.

But what if we can't fix our problem? Maybe we can't make the other person, place or thing change the way we want them to? Here again is where the Serenity Prayer is worth reviewing, and you may want to look again at the chapter on needing to be in control.

What if we have PTSD or other painful effects of trauma and we still can't find any peace? Here is where we can apply another and bigger formula: $R/H = GI + PI \times T + SP$

R/H (Recovery **+** Healing) **=** **GI** (Gather Information) **+ PI** (Process the Information) **x T** (over Time) **+ SP** (with Safe People).

As I have written in some detail in my prior books, we heal a little at a time by learning more about what happened to us (getting *more information*) and working it through alone and by talking about it with safe people over time (*processing* the information). By doing that, we can gradually develop more life skills to handle any future adversities—including core issues. If we take a step back, we may be able to see that it is our *observer self*—the part of us that is *watching* the whole scenario of events in our life unfold, including our feelings—and at the same time it (as we) is/are *experiencing* it all. When we are fully aware, this juxtaposition of the observer and experiencer gives us increased personal power. It does so by giving us more choices—such as what to do with our feelings and how to use them for whatever purpose we may find them to be most useful at the time. If we look at our life as being a movie, we can find that we are all at the same time the *author* of our story, the *producer*, *director*, *actor*, *experiencer*, and *co-creator* (with the God of our understanding). Knowing this gives us personal power to take responsibility for making our life go more peacefully and smoothly.

EMOTIONAL INTELLIGENCE [42]

What do feelings tell us? How can they be useful? My experience is that feelings are an important and complex part of our inner life. They become a core issue when they cause us undue emotional pain and distress and we cannot use them to our benefit—in short, when we cannot handle them constructively. Our feelings help tell us *what is going on inside* of us *or* what we *thought* or *sensed* was *going on outside* of us. Or some combination of both. They help us to be more aware of our life in each current moment. In that sense they give us information that may be *either* true or false, and that may help us in some way—or not.

Sometimes they are misleading, and giving too much attention to them may bring us more pain, grief and conflict, which I address below.

OBSERVATIONS ON FEELINGS

Carrol Izard found the following principles about feelings regarding their importance—and their potential complexity (expanded from my reading of the literature). [48, 49] Bear with me again, as some of this important information can be technical, but it is also practical.

1) Feelings (affect, emotions, etc.) are our **primary motivators** for our **thoughts** and **behavior**.

2) **Each** discrete feeling **serves distinct functions** in the way it **organizes** our *perception*, *cognition* (thinking), and *behavior* for the way we *adapt*, *cope* and *create* in our life.

3) Our feelings also **influence** our behavioral, cognitive and experiential **development** over the stages of our life.

4) These feeling-perception/cognition/behavior relations begin to **develop early** in our life and tend to remain stable over time, unless we begin to recognize, express and change some of them. **If a child is repeatedly traumatized, their ability to use their**

feelings in a healthy way as teens and adults is usually compromised.

5) The capacity of our feelings to *organize*, *motivate* and *sustain* particular ones or groups of our *behaviors* also contributes to the development of our *personality*.

6) Our *individual differences* in what Izzard called our "feelings activation thresholds" and in the frequency and intensity with which specific feelings are experienced are *major determinants* of our *personality* traits. [22]

This is a lot of information boiled down. Take a minute more and read these 6 principles again if you have time.

Experiential Exercise Answer these feelings questions below or elsewhere: What did you learn about feelings during your childhood, adolescence, and so far in your adult life?

_____

_____

_____

_____

What feelings did you see your parents or other authority figures express or talk about?

_____

_____

_____

What feelings do you tend to feel often now?

_____

_____

What might each mean?

_____
_____
_____
_____

What might each feeling mean *for you* when they come up?

_____
_____
_____

How do you usually handle them?

_____
_____
_____
_____

Have you taken any psychiatric drugs such as antidepressants and the like? How did they make you feel? _____

_____
_____

What feelings came up for you when you missed a dose or stopped taking them?

_____
_____

The following is a useful generic formula to explore our feelings further. It is often useful to fill in the blanks when we are in emotional pain.

**When _____ said/did _____ ,
I feel/felt _____, because _____**

12 NAMING AND HANDLING JOYFUL FEELINGS

Some divide feelings into "positive" and "negative." Since using these terms implies that it *is* or that it *may be* "good" or "bad" to have a particular feeling, I prefer to refer to them instead as **joy**ful and **pain**ful feelings. In this section and the next chapter I review some 17 kinds of feelings. Depending on the specific feeling, each of these has varying degrees of usefulness. In Figure 12.1 I list them from top to bottom according to the most joyful and useful to the most painful and least useful, depending on the context of what is happening inside and outside of us at the time.

JOYFUL FEELINGS

While feelings can be double-edged swords, I believe that **unconditional love** has essentially no downside. Its usefulness is that by feeling it toward a person, place or thing it allows us to feel safer whenever we may feel any pain of conflict or separation from them. Unconditional love thus heals that pain and generates optimism, positivity and usually a better sense of well-being.

FIGURE 12.1 ESTIMATE OF **NEGATIVE AND POSITIVE POTENTIAL** OF SOME BASIC FEELINGS

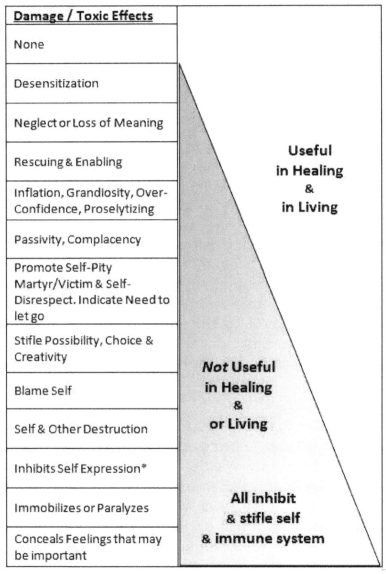

Damage / Toxic Effects	
None	
Desensitization	
Neglect or Loss of Meaning	
Rescuing & Enabling	**Useful in Healing & in Living**
Inflation, Grandiosity, Over-Confidence, Proselytizing	
Passivity, Complacency	
Promote Self-Pity Martyr/Victim & Self-Disrespect. Indicate Need to let go	
Stifle Possibility, Choice & Creativity	
Blame Self	**Not Useful in Healing & or Living**
Self & Other Destruction	
Inhibits Self Expression*	
Immobilizes or Paralyzes	**All inhibit & stifle self & immune system**
Conceals Feelings that may be important	

*Kills creativity, soul; sends Child Within into hiding.

FIGURE 12.1. ESTIMATE OF *POSITIVE* POTENTIAL
OF SOME BASIC FEELINGS (MATCH WITH LEFT CHART ROWS)

Feelings	Usefulness
Unconditional Love	Heals the separation; Allows feeling safe in separation
Joy	Realization of emotional completion
Compassion	Bonding, with freedom; helps both people in relationship with boundaries
Empathy	Felt connection, may be more limited than Compassion
Enthusiasm	Energy & motivation
Contentment	Sense of completion
Hurt Sadness	Indicate loss; Part of healing process of letting go
Emptiness Confusion	Space for creativity Opening; points to possibilities and choices
Guilt	Identify & handle mistakes
Anger Resentment	Boundaries and Limits Unfinished business
Shame	Humanness, limitation, vulnerability, humility, powerlessness
Fear	Warning: Being mistreated or about to be or just experienced or about to exp. loss
Numbness	Prevents early decompensation after a big loss

Spiritual masters—from Jesus to the Dalai Lama—have spoken of unconditional love's power, and *A Course in Miracles* describes it in detail. The psychologist Carl Rogers called it "Unconditional Positive Regard."

Joy—most briefly—is the realization of emotional completion. It is often associated with and results from our feeling unconditional love. Joy can be a kind of emotional feedback that we, our inner life and/or environment are on track, healthy or well. Many trauma survivors are often fearful of feeling joy because in their past whenever they felt it—or too much of it—something bad always happened. Its potential but uncommon hurtful or toxic side effect is desensitization to feeling other emotions.

"Happiness"—Notice that I do not include happiness in this list as a joyful feeling. This is because it is usually a combination or an amalgam of several joyful feelings while at the same time we are trying to handle and adapt to our painful ones and make some meaning of it all. Being in and working a full recovery program and enacting actions in the upper box in Figure 13.1 on page 148 usually facilitates this possibility into a reality. **Hope** is a desire and can be an aspect of some feelings. **Gratitude** often generates peace and/or joy.

Flow is the feeling experience of energized focus in a task or activity (and not on the chart) where we are fully involved, immersed, and successful in the process of the activity. It is an ideal feeling state for us when we are our most creative. Hungarian psychologist Mike Csikszentmihalyi has documented this joyful feeling across several areas of our life. [26]

We are most content or happy when in a flow state—a state of concentration or complete absorption with the activity at hand and the situation. It is an optimal state of intrinsic motivation, where we are fully immersed in what we are doing. This is a feeling everyone has at times, characterized by a feeling of great absorption, engagement, fulfillment, and skill—and during which temporal concerns (time, food, ego-self, etc) are typically ignored. We are completely involved in an activity for its own sake. The ego falls away. Time flies. The saying "Time flies when you're having fun" reminds us that being in the flow state is fun—something we trauma survivors may find difficult.*(see box next page) Every action, movement, and thought follows inevitably from the previous one, like playing jazz. Our whole being is involved, and we're using our skills to the utmost.

Flow is a completely focused motivation. It is a single-minded immersion in a creative endeavor and represents perhaps the ultimate in harnessing our emotions to perform and learn. In flow, our feelings are not just focused, but they are positive, energized, and

> * Closely related to flow, **Fun** is the enjoyment of pleasure and, according to Johan Huizinga, "an absolutely primary category of life, familiar to everybody at a glance right down to the animal level." Fun may be encountered in many human activities during work, social functions, recreation and play, and even seemingly mundane activities of daily living. The distinction between enjoyment and fun is difficult to articulate —but real, fun being a more spontaneous, playful, and active event. Fun is often described as doing *what you enjoy*, which can be almost any activity imaginable. [36, 37]

aligned with the task at hand. To be caught or stuck in sadness or fear we miss the peace and joy of flow. The hallmark of flow is a feeling of spontaneous joy when performing a task, while deeply focused on nothing but the activity—not even us or our emotions. Common terms for flow include: in the flow, the zone, the groove, the Now, the Tao, runner's high, the Holy Instant (from *A Course in Miracles*) or even fun. Historical sources hint that Michelangelo may have painted the ceiling of the Vatican's Sistine Chapel while in a flow state: painting for days at a time, absorbed in his work, not stopping for food or sleep until he reached the point of passing out. He would awake refreshed and, upon starting to paint again, re-entered a state of complete absorption. But most of us don't need to go that long to experience or appreciate it.

To achieve flow, we match our skill with the challenge of the task at hand. If the task is too easy or too difficult, flow cannot occur. Our skill level and challenge level must be matched and high; if skill and challenge are low and matched, then apathy results (Figure 12.2). The flow state also implies a kind of focused attention similar to mindfulness, meditation, yoga, and martial arts which improve our capacity for flow. Among other benefits, all of these activities train and improve attention. In short, flow could be described as a state where attention, motivation, and the situation meet, resulting in a kind of productive harmony. [26]

Compassion (Latin: "co-suffering") is emotional bonding with empathy and sympathy, yet with healthy boundaries and freedom from enmeshment.

A base for the highest principles in philosophy, society, and personhood, compassion is a feeling considered in all the major religions as a virtue. Here we sense the pain of others as a part of love itself. Promoting greater social harmony, it covers a wide spectrum from detachment to sympathy to empathy, as expanded in Figure A.1 at the end of the Appendix. Its only downside may be when we detach with love as in Al-Anon as appearing to neglect the other, when in most cases it is healthy to keep appropriate boundaries.

Empathy is a similar felt connection and may be seen as a useful part of compassion. [30,42,48,81,82] Its various dimensions cover a spectrum ranging from feeling a concern for another and often with a desire to help them, to experiencing emotions that match another's emotions, to sensing what another is thinking or feeling, to *knowing* emotionally what they are experiencing from their situation, to putting one's self in another's emotional shoes. Its downside is enmeshment and the grief we may experience when we are compelled to rescue or enable their behavior that got them there in the first place. Sociopaths (who have antisocial personality disorder) and child molesters aren't able to feel empathy.

Enthusiasm is a feeling of energy and motivation about something. It means intense enjoyment, interest, or approval. To be enthusiastic about something can give us a great advantage in many aspects of our life. It gives us energy and drive to finish a project, task or undertaking. Its downside can be ego-inflation, grandiosity, overconfidence and/or proselytizing.

Contentment is a felt sense of completeness or enjoyment of whatever we *already have* in our life. The more content we or our community become, the less extreme and more acceptable are usually our desires. If we let go, feel and enjoy, it can be self sustaining. It is an intuitive and natural state. Some refer to contentment as feeling **peace**. Feeling peaceful or being at peace can have two meanings: "peace" as 1) a general experience dependent on the *absence* of feeling restricted (e.g., as when living under socialism or communism), or during varying degrees of war, and 2) feeling relaxed and without fear. Some say happiness—which does not last—is not the goal, peace is. Contentment's downside can be a kind of negative complacency or passivity, as summarized in Figure 12.1 above.

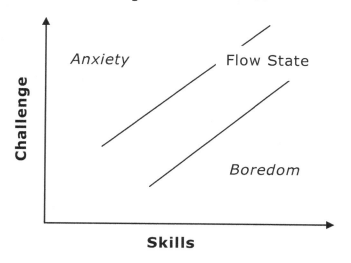

Figure 12.2. Flow State dynamics [26]

13   NAMING AND HANDLING PAINFUL FEELINGS

Growing up in a troubled family and world we may have been modeled and taught ineffective ways to handle emotional pain. A key to handling painful, distressing or unpleasant feelings is to *name* the feeling(s), *explore* and *find* what their *cause* may be, and then *address them*. [30,42,48, 81,82, 92]

PAINFUL FEELINGS

Hurt and/or **sadness** usually reflect a substantial loss, rejection or other trauma and are a normal and healthy part of grieving. These feelings are usually temporary and will pass especially when we name them and their cause accurately and then address the cause directly. Feeling them does not usually mean that we have "depression" or any other "mental illness." Their downside can come when we get stuck in them, feel self pity and shame for feeling them. Another common downside is that if you express these or similar painful feelings with some people, especially most clinicians, they or others may try to label you with a "mental illness" and try to drug you with toxic psychiatric drugs. [9,103]

Emptiness is a feeling that most people don't readily identify, but it is there continually in many of us. Here we feel as though we are missing something, as though we have a hole in our heart, and we usually want to fill it with something that makes our pain go away. A common part of the human condition, it can manifest as a sense of generalized boredom, social alienation and apathy. Feelings of emptiness *often accompany* loneliness, despair, or other painful states—from addictions to alcohol and other drugs to food to PTSD to chronic disabling illness.

A sense of emptiness is also part of a natural process of grief and grieving, as happens from serious relationship separation, the death of a loved one, or other significant loss. It may be the one painful feeling that so often subtly lingers deep in our inner life. The upside of emptiness is that it can be and is a *space from which creativity can emerge* if we reframe it in that direction. In our therapy and recovery process, identifying and working on it can give us a deeper and more powerful advantage as we heal. Its downside is that if we stay mired in it, it will stifle our possibility, choice, and creativity. The particular *meanings* of "emptiness" that we may give it vary with the context and the spiritual, religious or cultural tradition in which we experience and use it. An ultimate answer to healing from and with it can be to find and experience our real self and our felt connection to the God of our understanding. Knowing ourselves and God authentically usually fills our emptiness.

Confusion is when we feel unclear, not understanding, bewildered—and in the extreme—disoriented or even chaotic. It may span a spectrum from being unable to think with our usual speed or clarity to feeling disoriented to having difficulty paying attention, remembering, and making decisions. It can be caused by any number of conditions from taking toxic drugs that decrease mental clarity like heavy alcohol intake, antidepressant or antipsychotic drugs and the like to having various kinds of medical illness, including active PTSD, to sleep deprivation to ego attachment. Our ego likes us to stay confused so it can try to run our life. Whatever its cause, we—as our real self—can look for and find it and correct it.

Confusion's upside is that if we choose we can welcome it and use it to our advantage. That advantage is that it can give us an *opening*. It points to our exploring and finding potential *new possibilities* and *choices* regarding whatever issue or conflict that we may find ourself confused about. Its downside—as is for emptiness—is that if we stay mired in it, it will stifle our possibility, choice, and creativity.

Guilt is a painful feeling that we may get when we make a serious mistake. We feel bad when we do something wrong, or do not do something right. Its upside is that we can use it to correct our mistake and if needed, make amends to anyone who we may have wronged. Its downside is that if we stay mired in it we can continue to suffer with it indefinitely. If it persists, we can ask the God of our understanding to take it away—which is another dimension of "Let go and let God."

Sociopaths (who have narcissistic personality disorder) and child molesters aren't able to feel guilt, remorse or empathy. Remorse is a feeling of personal regret after committing an act which we consider shameful, hurtful, or violent. Remorse is closely allied to guilt and self-directed resentment.

Anger is a feeling we often get when we believe we have been offended, wronged or denied and we often have a tendency to try to undo that by retaliation. Anger's upside is that we can use it to *set healthy boundaries* and limits on any transgressors and correct any problems or deficiencies we may associate with any person, place or thing with whom we may be angry. It is also a key feeling that happens early in the *grieving process*. Its downside—if we hold on to it—can be self and other destruction and can turn into chronic and often insidious resentment. Frustration is usually a mixture of anger, fear and confusion.

There are three ways to show and express anger: aggressively, passively and constructively, for which I give several examples in Table 13.1. on the next 5 pages Study each item in this table and see which ways *you* may have used or have seen *others* use to express their anger. Look especially for any ways you may have noticed anyone use in your family of origin—since this may have been what was modeled for you and what you eventually may have learned to do yourself. Or you may have learned to do the opposite of what you saw, but perhaps that didn't work well for you. Then look at the kinds of *constructive* anger at the end of the table.

The "Four Faces of Anger" model can be yet another tool for understanding and accepting how natural and powerful expressing assertiveness and anger can be. And with enhanced awareness, hopefully, we can experience and communicate anger more responsibly and productively (more in chapter 16).

Table 13.2. Four Faces of Anger

Anger Type	Constructive	Destructive
• Purposeful	Assertive	Hostile
• Spontaneous	Passion	Rage

Table 13.1. Three Ways to Express Anger:
Aggressive, Passive, Constructive - next 5 pages

Aggressive Types	Examples of *Aggressive Anger*
Bullying	Threatening people directly, persecuting, pushing or shoving, using power to oppress, shouting, using a car to force someone off the road, playing on people's weaknesses.
Destructive Anger	Destroying objects, harming animals, destroying a relationship between two people, reckless driving.
Hurtful Anger	Physical violence, verbal abuse, strong sarcasm or teasing, inappropriate or vulgar jokes, repeated foul language, breaking a confidence, ignoring others' feelings, angry blaming, punishing people for unwarranted deeds, labeling others.
Threatening	Frightening people by saying how you could harm them, their property or their prospects, finger pointing, fist shaking, wearing clothes or symbols associated with violence, tailgating, excessive car horn blowing, slamming doors.
Unjust blaming	Accusing other people for your own mistakes, blaming people for your own feelings, making general accusations.

Aggressive Types	Examples of *Aggressive Anger*
Grandiosity	Showing off, expressing undue mistrust, not delegating, being a sore loser, wanting center stage, not listening, talking over others, expecting kiss & make-up to solve problems.
Manic behavior	Speaking too fast, excess energy, racing thoughts, working too much and expecting others to fit in, driving too fast, reckless spending, poor judgment.
Selfishness	Ignoring others' needs, not responding to requests for help, queue jumping.
Unpredictability	Explosive rages over minor frustrations, attacking indiscriminately, dispensing unjust punishment, inflicting harm on others for the sake of it, illogical arguments.
Vengeance	Being over-punitive, refusing to forgive and forget, bringing up hurtful memories from the past.

I describe *passive* types of anger starting on the next page.

Passive Types	Examples of *Passive Anger*
Evasiveness	Turning your back in a crisis, obsessively avoiding conflict, not arguing back, becoming phobic.
Dispassion	Giving the cold shoulder or phony smiles, looking unconcerned, withdrawing, dampening important feelings with alcohol or other drugs, overeating, oversleeping, not responding to another's anger, frigidity, talking of frustrations without showing feeling.
Psychological manipulation	Provoking people to aggression & then patronizing them, provoking aggression but staying on the sidelines, emotional blackmail, false tearfulness, feigning illness, sabotaging relationships, sexual provocation, using a third party to convey painful feelings (triangling), inappropriately withholding support, money or resources.
Obsessive behavior	Needing to be inordinately neat, clean and tidy, making a habit of constantly checking things, over-dieting or overeating, demanding that all jobs be done perfectly.

Passive Types	Examples of Passive Anger
Ineffectualness	Setting yourself & others up for failure, choosing unreliable people to depend on, being accident prone, underachieving, expressing frustration at insignificant things but ignoring serious ones.
Secretive behavior	Stockpiling resentments that are expressed behind people's backs, giving the silent treatment or under-the-breath mutterings, avoiding eye contact, putting people down, gossiping, anonymous complaints, poison pen letters, stealing, & conning.
Self-blame	Apologizing too often, being overly critical, inviting criticism.
Self-sacrifice	Being overly helpful, making do with second best, quietly making long-suffering signs but refusing help, or lapping up gratefulness from others.

I conclude this section with a summary of constructive types of anger on the next page.

Constructive Ways	Examples of Constructive Anger
Setting healthy boundaries	Setting healthy boundaries where others impinge on our space, freedom, privacy & the like.
Correcting errors	Correcting misunderstandings, misperceptions, misinformation, mistakes or the like.
Being Assertive	*Politely* expressing & getting what is ours or has been neglected or taken away from us.
Fair fighting	Fair and safe arguing about a difference in a couple or partnership (See in Appendix)
Settling a dispute	Using effective negotiating skills to get what we want or can.
Grieving	Expressing anger at having a major loss, such as a loved one or an important job (& then using our anger energy to get another job).
In therapy	Using supervised constructive anger bat ("bataka") work to move stuck grief.

As shown in Figure 12.2 in the previous chapter, so often—a large percentage of the time—**most** of these painful feelings are *not useful* to make our life *any better*. This includes anger and resentment. These are all too often not useful in promoting our recovery, wellbeing or living any better. If they persist, these painful feelings also can inhibit and stifle our real self and immune system. At the same time, to make our recovery and healing work we usually need to express and share these painful feelings with safe people such as our therapist, counselor, Twelve Step fellowship sponsor or our therapy group to see how we can best work them through. They are thus clearly double-edged swords, as I show below. Sometimes—if we use it right (as in Table 12.1 on page 122)—anger can be useful. But holding on to it too long may be hurtful to us and others. As we evolve in our healing process and work through each of our core issues we can slowly attain the wisdom to know the difference as to when and how to best use it and the other painful feelings. [92]

Resentment, as mentioned above, is chronic and often insidious. Paul Solomon tries to simplify: resentment is directed towards higher-status others, anger is directed towards peers and contempt is directed towards lower-status people. [81] Not that simple? Resentment can be draining. When unresolved, it can make us touchy or edgy when thinking of the resented one. We may deny our anger, yet get angry if others recognize them positively. It can result in a hostile, cynical, sarcastic attitude that can block healthy relationships, stunt personal and emotional growth, promote difficulty trusting and being real, and trigger addictions and shame. But resentment may not have any direct negative effects on the person we resent, save for the deterioration of the relationship.

Psychologist James Messina suggests five steps to healing resentments:

(1) Identify the resentment's source and what the other did to evoke it, (2) develop a new way of looking at our past, present and future life, including how it has affected us and how letting go of it can give us relief, (3) write an unmailed letter to the resented one, listing their offenses and how they hurt us, and read it to our therapist or counselor—ideally then doing expressive anger bat work with their supervision, and then if ready, let go of our resentment, (4) visualize a future without the resentment's negative effects, and (5) if resentment lingers, return to Step 1 and begin again.

Working Steps 4 & 5 and 8 & 9 of the Twelve Steps also helps letting go of resentments.

Shame is a key painful feeling. Shame is almost useless *unless* we use it constructively in our process of healing from trauma, some important aspects of which I begin to address in the next chapter.

Fear (aka "anxiety") is among the most common painful feelings. When we feel it we can enlist our personal power by calling it simply *fear* and *not* anxiety or panic, and *find its cause* and then *address* that. Fear is often a *warning* that we are about to lose something or that we are about to be mistreated (shamed, threatened or harmed), misunderstood or rejected. It is a normal reaction to a real or imagined threat or loss. Some differentiate *fear* as an emotional response to a current perceived threat or danger, from *anxiety* which they say is related to future situations perceived as uncontrollable or unavoidable. I see calling it "anxiety" instead of fear as *mystifying* it as though it were some vague emotional pain that we have neither responsibility for bringing about or ability to handle. The two are essentially identical in emotional experience, except that calling it fear *de*mystifies it and makes it easier to handle for most people.

Fear has four major parts: **emotional** (painful apprehension, tension, expecting the worst, feeling irritable, restless, watching for danger, panic [feeling as though we are about to die or pass out]), **cognitive** (**thinking**) (worry, uneasiness, trouble concentrating and dread), **physical** (heart palpitations, muscle weakness and tension, fatigue, nausea, chest pain, shortness of breath, abdominal pain, headaches), and **behavioral** (withdrawal from fearful situations, insomnia, nail biting and nervous tension, such as foot shaking). When excessive, unaware clinicians may misdiagnose it as a simple anxiety or panic disorder and not look for its *cause*. The most common treatable causes that I have seen assisting people over the years is PTSD, frequent age regressions and psychiatric drug toxicity, including drug withdrawal. Sedative drugs to lessen it are shortcuts for serious emergencies only and for about only a day or two, otherwise chemical dependence will set in and the fear will worsen as drug withdrawal makes it all worse. Most of the time that we feel it excessively—and don't address its cause—we are wasting our time and energy.

Paul Tillich saw *existential* anxiety as "the state in which a being is aware of its possible nonbeing" and he listed three categories for the nonbeing and resulting anxiety: *ontic* (fate and death), *moral* (guilt and condemnation), and *spiritual* (emptiness and meaninglessness). According to Tillich, the last of these three types of existential anxiety, i.e., spiritual anxiety, is predominant in modern times, while the others were predominant in earlier periods. He argues that this anxiety can be accepted as part of the Human Condition or it can be resisted, but with negative consequences. In its pathological form, spiritual anxiety may tend to "drive the person toward the creation of certitude in systems of meaning which are supported by tradition and authority" even though such "undoubted certitude is not built on the rock of reality."

According to Viktor Frankl, the author of *Man's Search for Meaning*, when a person is faced with extreme mortal dangers, the most basic of all human wishes is to find a meaning of life to combat the "trauma of nonbeing" as death is near. (We make meaning in Stages 2 and 3 recovery.)

Numbness is an inability to feel the above normal feelings. It is common among trauma survivors and people prescribed psychiatric drugs who don't know that it is *not wise* to take them for several reasons, including the emotional numbness that they routinely cause. In both of these situations, numbness is the usual underlying state that people experience—with an occasional outburst of overwhelming pain, especially if drug withdrawal happens. [9] Of course, this emotional roller coaster effect is routinely misdiagnosed as "bipolar" or some other "mental illness." [103]

Numbness is so seldom discussed or studied and written about that there is little professional knowledge about it—yet it remains a common painful feeling. The main way psychology and psychiatry appear to understand it is to call it *alexithymia*, which means "no words for emotion," from the Greek **a** for "lack", **lexis** for "word" and **thymia** for "emotion." Apparently knowing little about its two main causes (trauma and psychiatric drug effects) they believe that it is a real disorder characterized by the inability to identify and verbally describe emotions and feelings in oneself and others. This erroneous belief allows them *not* to take a thorough trauma history while drugging the person into more numbness for any other psychological or psychiatric symptom that they may disclose. Numbness is not the simple absence of all feelings. It is a painful and confusing experience that stifles our peace and creativity over a long time unless and until we begin a serious recovery. The only upside of this painful feeling is when it is a normal part of healthy grieving. Its downside is when it cancels feelings that may be important.

Low energy is related to numbness and is almost never mentioned as a painful feeling, yet most of us feel it too often. It is the *opposite* of the *flow state* and is commonly felt in combination with several of the above painful feelings. These low energy states may include: 1) "depression," 2) waking up in the morning slower than we want, 3) after having a bad night's sleep, 4) *taking* psychiatric drugs (antidepressants, antipsychotics, and sedatives [such as benzodiazepines and "mood stabilizers,"]) as well as 5) *withdrawal* from *these* and 6) *withdrawal* from stimulant drugs (nicotine, caffeine, Ritalin, amphetamines, cocaine and the like) or opiates wherein we usually want a quick pick-me-up in the form of our drug of choice or another drug. [103]

Low energy is also commonly experienced as 7) a part of PTSD that is often misdiagnosed as "depression" and other "mental disorders." It is sometimes found associated with 8) medical illnesses such as hypothyroidism, infections as Lyme disease, some viral illness as herpes zoster, and chronic fatigue syndrome and fibromyalgia. Low energy is nearly universal as 9) a part of *normal* healthy grieving when we experience a major loss or trauma, and it is often 10) associated with an unhealthy lifestyle (nicotine intake, eating junk food, alcohol and other drug misuse, promiscuity, and other high risk behavior). Finally, it is common when we have too much happening around us which can distract us from our focus. Every second a lot of environmental information is coming to us through our senses. Our mind can attend to only a certain amount of information at a time. According to Miller's classic 1956 study, that number is about 126 bits of information per second. That may seem like a large number (and a lot of information), but simple daily tasks take quite a lot of information. Just having a conversation takes about 40 bits of information per second; that's 1/3 of one's capacity. [69] That is why when we are having a conversation we cannot focus as much of our attention on other things.

Look carefully at the two levels in Figure 13.1. Study it and see if any of its situations or experiences you may be in *now* and whether you may ever want to be in another one or more of them instead. A common situation for many—*before* achieving a sizeable recovery—is to be somewhere in the lower box, *not* a peaceful place to be. But once we get stuck there, we may get so used to being in pain that we don't think we can ever get free of it. To rise up to the top level with its distinct advantages of being able to access a flow state more easily, we can begin a recovery program at whichever stage we may find ourself (Table A.2. on page 270 in the Appendix).

The fact that you are holding this book in your hands and reading these words may indicate that you have an interest in getting free of the pain associated with repeated lower box situations.

So how can you get any peace? A way out is to name our pain and core issues and work through them as summarized in the first two chapters and described throughout this book.

FIGURE 13.1 AWAKENING TO HEALING AND CHOOSING IT

After
- Regular exercise
- Healthy diet and nutrition
- Daily meditation , adequate sleep
- Healthy reframing and optimism in conflicts
- Look for missing information regarding emotional pain and ways to reframe it
- Working recovery program, incl. core issues
- Avoid psychiatric (or other toxic) drugs
- Contentment and **peace more often** than not will likely slowly result

 Awakening to Healing

Before
- Unhealthy lifestyle (nicotine intake, eating junk food, alcohol and other drug misuse, unsafe sex/promiscuity, and other high risk behavior)
- Misdiagnosed with "mental illness" and mistreated with toxic drugs
- Take psychiatric drugs such as antidepressants, antipsychotics, benzodiazepine sedatives and "mood stabilizers"
- Frequent and bothersome worrying
- Difficulty sleeping
- Chronic fatigue   Result: **Painful life ongoing**

GETTING MORE ENERGY & INTO THE FLOW STATE

Having described principles of feelings and the common joyful and painful ones above, let's look at some practical ways to get more energy and into a flow state (Table 13.3). Look over the table and see which entry way you have used and which you might consider using more.

TABLE 13.3. WAYS TO INITIATE OR TRIGGER ENERGY AND A FLOW STATE

Categories	*Ways* to *initiate* or *trigger* *energy* and a flow state
Physical	Regular exercise, healthy diet & nutrition, *avoid* psychiatric (or other toxic) drugs, good sleep [103]
Mental	Remember that we can enter flow at almost any time; daily meditation, healthy reframing & optimism in conflicts & core issues, look for any missing information that may be causing you emotional pain (see p 114 above)
Emotional	Having wisdom to know the difference between useful & useless emotional pain (Figure 12.1 above) & how to handle it
Spiritual	Daily prayer and meditation, Living here now

Remember that we can enter flow at almost any time. We just have to decide to do so and then choose to enter it. If needed, look for any *missing information* that may be causing you emotional pain and distracting you from getting into flow (page 114).

Easy irritability, fear, anxiety, anger, restlessness, sometimes feeling as though we are on an "emotional roller coaster," confusion —and insomnia— are common symptoms of withdrawal from psychiatric and *other* psychoactive drugs —from alcohol to all the rest, including legal psychiatric drugs.[9] These are also manifestations of active PTSD. [103]

The secret of life is creating energy, then managing it, optimally.
— Michael Grant White

For more on how to address and handle anger and resentments, see the second half of Chapter 16.

As I noted before, shame is almost useless unless we use it constructively in our process of healing from trauma, some important aspects of which I begin to address in the next chapter.

14 LOW SELF ESTEEM / SHAME

Low self esteem is both a painful feeling *and* a core issue that is more efficiently called shame. [32, 34, 55, 58, 61, 72, 73, 103]

Shame has many guises. If shame is the umbrella, its spokes are low self-esteem or self-worth, shyness, easy embarrassment, self-deprecation, self-hate, and at times the seeming opposites of arrogance and/or grandiosity and more. It reflects that we may have a decreased awareness of our true self, which we usually have lost when we feel it. Our lost selfhood is probably the most hurtful effect of repeated childhood trauma. Two of the more related, unifying and core experiences of trauma are the effect of PTSD, and a pervasive, underlying belief and feeling of shame. Burdened with shame, we may not be able to care for ourself in a healthy way. Because it is so pervasive and toxic, I will spend a little more time on it now, first contrasting it with guilt.

Shame is an uncomfortable or painful feeling that we experience when—consciously or unconsciously—we sense that a part of us is defective, bad, incomplete, inadequate, rotten, phony or a failure. In contrast to **guilt**, where we feel bad from *doing* something wrong, we feel **shame** from believing that we are *being* something wrong or bad. Thus guilt seems to be correctable or forgivable, whereas there may seem to be no way out of shame (see also page 133 on guilt in the prior chapter). Our true self feels the shame and when appropriate can express it in a healthy way to safe and supportive people. Our false self, on the other hand, pretends not to have the shame and would never tell anyone about it.

Shame is universal to the human condition. We *all* have some shame. Its only healthy form is humility. [100] If we don't work through it and then let go of it, shame tends to accumulate and often burdens us more over time, until we become its victim. In addition to feeling defective or inadequate, shame makes us believe that others can see through us, through our facade, and into our defectiveness. Shame feels hopeless: that no matter what we do, we cannot correct it. With shame we feel isolated and lonely, as though we are the only one who has it. While we often keep it buried, out of our conscious awareness, it still shows up and distracts us from our ability to feel peace and joy.

We may say, "I'm afraid to tell you about my shame because if I do, you'll think I'm bad, and I can't stand hearing how bad I am." And so not only do I keep it to myself, but I often block it out or pretend that it is not there. I may even *disguise* my shame as if it were some other feeling or action and then *project* that *onto other people*, including those who are close to me (see also Charles Finn's poem above on page 42). Some of these feelings and actions that may cover up, *mask* or *bind* our shame include:

GUISES OF SHAME

**• Anger • Resentment • Contempt
• Rage • Attack • Blame
• Control • Neglect/withdrawal
• Perfectionism • Abandonment
• Compulsive behavior**

(note how the other core issues throughout this book also intertwine with shame)

And when I feel or act out any of these guises of shame, that serves a useful purpose for my co-dependent or false self—acting as a defense against my feeling ashamed. But, even though I may defend myself well against my shame, it can still be seen by others, e.g., when I hang my head, slump down, avoid eye contact, wear sunglasses indoors, hair over my eyes, or make apologies for having my feelings, needs, wants, and rights. I may even feel somewhat nauseated, cold, withdrawn and alienated. But no matter how well I may defend myself and others against it, my shame will not go away—unless I *learn what* it is, *name it accurately* when I encounter it, *experience* it more *consciously* and *share* it with *safe* and *supportive others*. The best place to do this is in ongoing individual or group therapy and self-help fellowship meetings.

WHERE DOES OUR SHAME COME FROM?

Our shame seems to come from what we do with the negative messages, negative thoughts, beliefs and rules that we hear, see and experience as we grow up in a troubled family and world. We hear and experience these abuses from our parents, parent figures, and other people in authority, such as teachers, bosses and clergy. These messages basically tell us that we are somehow not okay that our feelings, our needs, our true self or child within are not acceptable. Our real self takes in all that shame while it stays in hiding.

Over and over, we hear messages like "shame on you!" "You're so bad!" "You're not good enough!" We hear them so often, and from people on whom we are so dependent and to whom we are so vulnerable, that we believe them. And so we incorporate or internalize them into our very being.

As if that were not enough, the wound is compounded by negative rules that stifle and prohibit the otherwise healthy healing and needed expression of our pains. Rules like "Don't feel," "Don't cry" and "Children are to be seen and not heard." And so not only do we learn that we are bad, but that we are not to talk openly about any of it.

However, these negative rules are often inconsistently enforced. The result? Difficulty in trusting rule-makers and authority figures, and we feel fear, guilt, and more shame. And where do our parents learn these negative messages and rules? Most likely from *their* parents and other authority figures. This is another example of childhood trauma (here as emotional abuse) being transmitted from one generation to the next. (See page 47 of my book *Healing the Child Within* for a list of negative rules and messages commonly heard in troubled families.)

THE SHAME-BASED FAMILY

When everyone in a dysfunctional family comes from and communicates with others from a common practice of shaming, it can be described as shame-based. Parents in such a family did not have their needs met as infants and children and usually as they continue into adulthood as well. They often use their children to meet many of these unmet needs. [68,103]

Shame-based families often, though not always, have a *secret*. This secret may span all kinds of "shameful" events or conditions, from family violence to sexual abuse to alcoholism to having been in prison or a concentration camp or having a relative who was. Or the secret may be as subtle as a lost job, a lost promotion or a lost relationship. Keeping such secrets disables all members of the family, whether or not they know the secret. This is because being secretive prevents the expression of questions, concern and feelings (such as fear, anger, shame and guilt). And the family thus cannot communicate freely. And the true self/child within each family member remains stifled— unable to grow and develop.

RECOVERY AIDS FOR HEALING SHAME

In my work assisting trauma survivors in their recovery I have observed an almost universal finding of low self-esteem among them. The belief and painful feeling of shame declares that "I am bad, not enough, flawed, inadequate, imperfect and even rotten at my core." Shame appears to be taught and learned, repeatedly implanted by abusers, which their victims incorporate into their beings. This subtle yet toxic process often begins at birth and can continue as repeated child abuse, and more traumas may be repeated throughout an adult's life. Active shame blocks healing.

Shame v Guilt - *in Review* A recovery program can slowly address and heal the effects of trauma, including the shame. Primary in healing shame is first to *name it* accurately, in whatever guise it may appear (Figure 13.1 summarizes many of them). *Naming things accurately* gives us *personal power*. In review from above: it is important to differentiate shame from guilt. Sometimes confused with shame, **guilt** is a painful feeling that comes from making a mistake, *doing* something wrong—or not doing it right. We can heal guilt by apologizing or making amends to the person we may have wronged, and, if appropriate, perhaps even asking for forgiveness. Guilt is about doing or not doing.

Shame is about being or not being. In guilt, we have *done* something wrong which we can more easily correct. In shame, we feel and even think as though we *are* something wrong, and we can see no way to correct it. Often fostered by some organized religions as "original sin," we feel as though we are born defective and bad. From this collective shaming trauma, our false self/ego then maintains the shame. As one patient said, "I have a tape recorder in my head that reminds me of how bad I am."

FIGURE 14.1 GUISES OF SHAME (CONTINUED) [103]

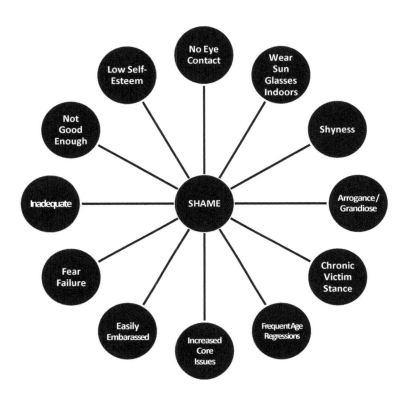

Another said, "There is this constant broadcast in the pit of my being telling me I'm not good enough." Shame can be so pervasive that it can stop people from going into recovery because they believe they don't deserve to, or that they will never feel better.

Shame is almost useless for us to feel (as shown in Figure 12.1 in Chapter 12 above) unless we use it constructively in our process of healing from trauma. A major way to heal shame is to *share our experience* of it with *safe people*. [103] An effective way to do that is to tell our story or narrative, bit by bit, of what happened to us in our trauma experiences. This process may be accomplished in individual therapy or counseling, during heart-to-heart talks with a trusted and safe friend, and in group therapy or a self-help group. Each time that we share our shame with safe people, we express it, and thereby expel it outside of ourself. Safe others witness us expressing it. By doing so, we paradoxically own that we experienced it, the others understand and accept our experience with it—with empathy and compassion—and then we can get rid of it. We *release what we know, understand* and we *express it*. Shame usually takes repeated sharing over a long time to heal. If someone *believes* that they are *mentally ill*, doing so may *aggravate* and compound that shame. Shame will likely rear its subtle but ugly head numerous times during recovery. However, participating in a recovery program will eventually affirm our inherent goodness as we heal from the toxic effects of shame.

15   GRIEVING

Losses and traumas are so common and subtle that we often do not recognize them. Yet most of them produce varying degrees of emotional pain: we call this pain and train of feelings grief. We can also call it the grieving process. When we allow ourselves to *feel* these painful feelings, give them an *accurate name*, and when we *share* our grief with *safe* and *supportive* others over time, we are able to complete our grief work and thus be free of it.

Grieving is a common way we experience and process our painful feelings after a significant hurt, loss or trauma. It may be one of the most important natural experiences that we can have, yet unfortunately it usually gets blocked or shut down from repeated trauma's stifling effects on us. We grieve our traumas periodically, from time to time, all of our life—if we are awake to our inner life. We should be able and allowed to process or metabolize our grief by expressing it in three situations: with safe others, when we are alone and with the God of our understanding. If we are awake to our inner life, *acute* grief is usually easier to work through. I summarize the common stages of grief in Table 15.1 In the middle column of the table I describe the usual parts and sequence of normal healthy grieving of an acute or *current* loss or trauma. We may not experience all of these parts or in this exact order. In the table read the summary description of each of these carefully.

As a child or adult, our active grief work was sometimes delayed. This was when we were so often repeatedly traumatized that we couldn't finish grieving one trauma before we were hit with another. And then another. As a helpless child it was unsafe to tell most others around us about our pain, even if we knew how and wanted to. Our focus may have been on just surviving. So we accumulate the painful and disruptive effects of one trauma after another and end up with what feels like a ton of unmetabolized and ungrieved grief, and we never get to heal it. I call this unfinished business *stuck grief*. Another term for it is PTSD. Both stuck grief and PTSD show essentially the same symptoms and signs as "depression," which is commonly misdiagnosed in trauma survivors. Enter our current "mental health" system and you will get a toxic antidepressant drug for your ungrieved grief. If you don't respond to the antidepressant, you will likely get more and/or an antipsychotic —even though you are not psychotic. And these drugs often make you worse. Has anything like that ever happened to you or to anyone you may know?

TABLE 15.1 PARTS OF NORMAL HEALTHY GRIEVING OF AN ACUTE LOSS OR TRAUMA* [80B]

Part or Component	Description	If Grief is Delayed** Common for adult trauma survivors
Shock, alarm, numbness, denial	Some experience this, & others don't. Some can express their pain immediately	Can last for years & manifest as other illness*
Preoccupation with the hurt, loss, trauma or conflict	Usual. Despite efforts to think of or do other things, it may be hard to focus on anything else.	Without grief work, the emotional pain usually smolders. *Common* – traumatic amnesia; often tries to fill the emptiness with PPTs.
Emotional release	Crying, anger, guilt, shame. Helpless, hopeless, low energy (see above). Age regressions. May manifest in unhealthy ways. Expressing the pain helps.	Sharing with safe others brings healthy grieving. Usually takes patience & a long time.

- - -

Wisdom to Know The Difference

Part or Component	Description	If Grief is Delayed** Common for adult trauma survivors
Physical symptoms *May occur anytime*	Sleeplessness. Throat tightness, choking feeling, shortness of breath, deep sighing. Empty feeling in chest or abdomen. Weakness, low appetite, GI problems.	Chronic medical problems (often unexplained), aches & pains are common.
Resolution and Integration	*If Resolved*: Search for meaning; acceptance; improved health & life quality; growth; new identity. *Unresolved*: Emotional & physical pain continues; vulnerable to more trauma & illness.	

*Any of these findings can be and are commonly misunderstood and mislabeled as "depression" or another "mental illness." [103]

**If from repeated childhood or later trauma that is still not grieved to resolution.
PPTs = People, places & things (such as drugs including alcohol, & nicotine).

In the right-hand column of Table 15.1 above I summarize how we can begin to grieve if we have stuck grief and/or PTSD. Take another minute and read this column carefully. Then read the notes under the table. To heal from these trauma effects of stuck grief and/or PTSD, we can begin a recovery program, part of which includes working on and through our core recovery issues, and when appropriate, beginning to grieve. To start, we can *name* the *trauma* or traumas that we have experienced. Then we can find *safe people* with whom we can *share our story* and our *grief*. Safe places to share include with: 1) a therapist or counselor, 2) a self help group such as Adult Children of Alcoholics/Trauma (ACA), Co-dependents Anonymous (CoDA), or Emotions Anonymous (EA), 3) a trauma-focused therapy group, and 4) a safe close friend who just listens and doesn't try to change us. We can also strengthen our recovery by 5) writing regularly in a journal or diary (keep it in a safe place). Be patient with all this.

Our healing takes a long time. The bigger the loss, the longer the time generally required. For a *minor* loss we may complete most of the grieving in a few hours, days or sometimes weeks. For a *moderate* loss this work may require weeks to months or longer. And for a *major* loss the time required for the healthy completion of grieving is usually from two to four years, or longer.

DOWNSIDE OF UNRESOLVED GRIEF

Emotional pain and PTSD: Unresolved grief festers like a deep wound covered by scar tissue, a pocket of vulnerability ever ready to break out anew. [80b] When we experience a loss or trauma, it stirs up energy within us that needs to be discharged. When we do not discharge this energy, the stress builds up to a state of chronic distress. Trauma savvy clinicians and researchers call it PTSD. With no release this chronic distress is stored within us as discomfort or tension that may at first be so subtle that it is difficult for us to recognize it. We may feel or experience it through a wide range of manifestations such as chronic fear, anxiety, tension or nervousness, anger or resentment, sadness, emptiness, unfulfillment, confusion, guilt, shame or, as is common among many who grew up in a troubled family, as a feeling of numbness. These feelings usually come and go. There may also be difficulty sleeping, aches, pains and other somatic complaints, and full-blown mental, emotional or physical illness, including PTSD. In short, we pay a price when we are not allowed to and do not grieve in a complete and healthy way.

Re-enactments: If we suffered losses in our childhood for which we were not allowed to grieve, we may grow up carrying several of the above conditions into and throughout our adulthood. We may also develop a tendency toward self-destructive or other-hurtful behaviors. These destructive behaviors may cause us and others unhappiness, get us into trouble and can cause us crisis after crisis. When these behaviors are repeated, they may be called a re-enactment or "repetition compulsion." It is as if we have an unconscious drive or compulsion to keep repeating one or more of these behaviors, even though they are not usually in our best interest. On the upside, we can *reframe* these re-enactments as manifestations of pain that are helping us work toward healing.

Children who grew up in a troubled or dysfunctional family suffer numerous losses over which they are often unable to grieve in a complete way. The many negative messages that we get when we try to grieve set up a major block: not feeling (numbness) and not talking about the trauma and pain. When these patterns that are learned as children and adolescents continue into adulthood, they are difficult to change. Yet in healing our Child Within, in finding, nurturing and being our True Self, we can change these ineffective behaviors and occurrences. In doing so we begin to break free of the bonds of our repeated and unnecessary confusion and suffering. We first have to identify and name our losses or traumas. Then we can begin to re-experience them, going through our grief work and completing it, rather than trying to go around it or avoid it—as we may have been doing up until now.

BEGINNING TO GRIEVE

We can begin our grief work through any of several possible ways. Some of these ways include beginning to:

1) Identify (i.e., accurately name) our hurts, losses or traumas.
2) Identify our needs that we may not have had met.
3) Identify our feelings and share them.
4) Work on this and other core issues.
5) Work a recovery program.

IDENTIFYING OUR LOSSES AND TRAUMAS

Identifying a hurt, loss or trauma may be difficult, especially one that we may have forgotten (by traumatic or dissociative amnesia), "stuffed," repressed or suppressed. Identifying one that happened long ago may be even more difficult. While talking about our pain and our concerns may be helpful, simple talking or "talk therapy" may take a while —and it may not be enough to activate feelings or grief around our ungrieved traumas.

That is why experiential therapy or techniques can be so helpful in activating and facilitating grief work. Experiential techniques, such as group therapy, telling our real story and journaling, allow a focus and a spontaneity that taps into the unconscious processes which otherwise may remain hidden from our ordinary awareness. Only an estimated 12% of our life and our knowledge is in our conscious awareness, in contrast to 88% that is in our unconscious. These experiential techniques are helpful not only in identifying, but also in doing our actual work of grieving. The following are examples of some experiential techniques that may be used to heal from our trauma effects through grieving our ungrieved hurts, losses or traumas.

1) Risking and sharing, especially feelings, with safe and supportive people.
2) Storytelling (telling our own story, including risking, and sharing).
3) Working through transference (what we project or "transfer" onto others).
4) Psychodrama, Gestalt Therapy, Family Sculpture.
5) Hypnosis and related techniques
6) Attending self-help meetings.
7) Working the Twelve Steps (of Al-Anon, ACA, AA, NA, CoDA, OA, EA, etc.).

8) Group therapy (usually a safe and supportive place to practice many of these experiential techniques)
9) Couples therapy or family therapy
10) Guided Imagery
11) Breathwork
12) Affirmations
13) Dream analysis
14) Art, Movement and Play therapy
15) Active imagination and using intuition
16) Meditation and Prayer
17) Therapeutic bodywork
18) Keeping a journal or diary

These experiential techniques should be used in the context of a full recovery program, ideally under the guidance of a therapist or counselor who knows these principles of healing. To help further in identifying our losses, especially our ungrieved ones, I have compiled some examples of losses (Table 15.2 below). This list can be supplemented by also re-reading or referring to Table 5, which describes some terms for various losses or traumas that we may have experienced as children and as adults.

A loss may be sudden, gradual or prolonged. It can be partial, complete, uncertain or unending. It can occur singly or be multiple and cumulative. Always personal, it may also be symbolic.

Loss is such a universal experience, but because we encounter it so often, we easily and often overlook it. Yet it always carries with it a threat to our self-esteem. Indeed, loss occurs any time [80b] we suffer a blow to our self-esteem.

While loss often occurs separately and discreetly, its resulting grief brings up prior ungrieved losses that have been stored in our unconscious. An ungrieved loss remains forever alive in our unconscious, which has no sense of time. Thus past losses or even a reminder of the loss, just as current losses or the memory of past losses, evoke fear of further loss in the future. [80b]

In summary, past losses and separations have an impact on current losses, separations and attachments. And all of these factors bear on fear of future losses and our capacity to make future attachments.[80b] Identifying an ungrieved loss is a beginning of getting free of its often painful hold on us.

Stages of Grief Acute grief tends to follow an approximate course, beginning with shock, fear, anxiety, easy distractibility and anger, progressing through more pain and despair. Psychiatrist John Bowlby said that eventually it ends on either a positive or a negative note, depending on the conditions around the loss and the person's opportunity to grieve it.

TABLE 15.2. SOME EXAMPLES OF LOSS
(Compiled from B. Simos 1979) [80b]

• An Important Person—Close or Meaningful Relationships
• Separation, divorce, rejection, desertion, abandonment, death, abortion, stillbirth, illness, geographic move, children leaving home, etc.
• Part of Ourself (Real Self, self esteem, self worth; spiritual self)
• Body image, accident, loss of function, illness, loss of control, self-esteem, independence, ego, expectations, lifestyle, needs, culture-shock, job change, expectations, hopes, beliefs, etc.
• Childhood, an abuse and neglect free one
• Healthy parenting, getting needs met, healthy development (through stages), transitional objects (blanket, soft toy, etc.), gain or loss of siblings or other family members, body changes (e.g., in adolescence, middle age and older age).
• Threats of loss; separation or divorce.
• Adult Developmental Transitions, including mid-life and older life.
• External Objects, e.g., Money, property, necessities (keys, wallet, etc.), car, sentimental objects, collections.
• Instant altered state of consciousness and/or pain relief (the alcohol or the drug or the adrenaline high)

These stages or phases may be further described by breaking them down into more detailed components. [80b]

Stage 1. Shock, alarm, denial and the above findings.

Stage 2. Acute grief, consisting of:

• Continuing, intermittent, and lessening denial. Physical and psychological pain and distress. Contradictory pulls, emotions and impulses. Searching behavior composed of: preoccupation with thoughts of the loss, a compulsion to speak of the loss, and to retrieve that which was lost, a sense of waiting for something to happen, aimless wandering and restlessness, a feeling of being lost, of not knowing what to do, inability to initiate any activity, a feeling that time is suspended, disorganization and a sense that life can never be worthwhile again, confusion and feelings that things are not real, fear that all the above indicate mental illness.

• Crying, anger, guilt, shame. Identifying with traits, values, symptoms, tastes or characteristics of the lost object.

• Regression or return to behaviors and feelings of an earlier age or connected with a previous loss or reactions thereto. Helplessness and depression, hope or hopelessness, relief.

Eventually: Decrease in pain and increasing capacity to cope over time. A drive to find meaning in the loss. Beginning thoughts of a new life without the lost object.

Stage 3. *Integration* of the loss and grief. *If* the *outcome* is *favorable*: Acceptance of the reality of the loss and return to physical and psychological well-being, diminished frequency and intensity of crying, restored self-esteem, focus on the present and future, ability to enjoy life again, pleasure at awareness of growth from the experience, reorganization of a new identity with restitution for the loss and loss remembered with poignancy and caring instead of pain.

If the outcome is *un*favorable: Acceptance of the reality of the loss with lingering sense of low energy ("depression" and physical aches and pains, lower self-esteem, reorganization of a new identity with constriction of personality and involvement and vulnerability to other separations and losses. [80b]

Breaking these stages down into these components helps us understand the grief process. However, these components are not discrete and sequential. They don't always happen in any prescribed order. Rather, they tend to *overlap* and to *move around* the various areas and manifestations listed above.

Dana was a 28-year-old woman who grew up in an abusive and actively alcoholic family. In her late teens she became alcoholic, and four years ago, at age 24, she stopped drinking and began treatment for her alcoholism. She had been in our therapy group for adult children of alcoholics and other troubled families for about two years, making noticeable progress. When she broke up with her boyfriend, she told the group, "I'm hurting so bad. I'm down to my last hurt, this emptiness is so bad. I broke up with my boyfriend two weeks ago. This week I started crying and just couldn't stop. I'm realizing that breaking up is not all that is making me feel so bad. It is my loss of that little girl inside of me. I've been going home every night and crying myself to sleep." Here she cries, and takes a long pause. "I just can't believe that that little girl was treated as bad as she was. But it's true."

In beginning to grieve over one loss—the relationship with her boyfriend—she triggered her unfinished grieving over another loss—the mistreatment and abuse of her Child Within. This is an example of how grieving is not always as simple as it might first appear. Of course, Dana had been grieving the loss of her Child Within for a long time, although it was in an incomplete way, including through the repetition compulsion of going out with men who mistreated her, by not trusting her sponsor in A.A. and not trusting the therapy group for nearly the first year of her joining it. But gradually she began to risk and to tell her true story little by little. She is now beginning to break free of the shackles of her false self (ego) and her repetition compulsion and to heal.

To work through the pain of our grieving, we experience all of our feelings as they come up for us, without trying to change them. Grief is active work. It is mental and emotional labor, exhaustive and exhausting. [80b] It is so painful that we often try to avoid the pain around it. Some ways that we may try to avoid grieving include:

• Continuing to deny the loss.
• Intellectualizing about it.
• Stuffing our feelings.
• Macho mentality (I'm strong;
   I can handle it myself).
• Using alcohol/other drugs, incl. psychiatric;
• Prolonged attempts to get the lost object
   back or other addictions/attachments.

Even though we may get temporary relief by such methods, not feeling and working through our grief only prolongs our pain. Overall, we can consume as much energy in *avoiding* grieving as we would if we went ahead and grieved our loss or trauma. When we feel something as we grieve, we decrease its power over us. We may discover that we have been avoiding grief work over losses or traumas that happened a long time ago. Yet we suffered much and long through our inability to grieve. For some of us it may now be time to begin to work through and to complete our grieving.

16   TELLING OUR STORY, GRIEVING & CORE ISSUES

In the previous chapter I listed risking and sharing, especially feelings, with safe and supportive people as a way to facilitate grieving. Doing so makes it easier to identify and work through all of the core issues. When we risk, we expose our Real Self. We take a chance and we become vulnerable. When we do this, two opposites may emerge— acceptance or rejection. Whatever we may decide to risk about ourself, another may accept or reject—or they may react somewhere in between.

Many of us may have been so wounded from risking—whether in our childhood, adolescence, adulthood or all three—that we are usually reluctant or unable to risk and share our Real Self with others. Yet we are caught in a dilemma: when we hold in our feelings, thoughts, concerns and creativities, our Real Self becomes stifled and we feel bad, we hurt. Our held-in energy may build up so much that the only way we can handle it is to let it out to someone. This is the predicament that many of us who grew up in troubled families encounter. And because of a number of factors, such as our seeking approval, validation, excitement and intimacy, we may select someone who is not safe and supportive. Indeed, they may reject us or betray us in some way, which may just confirm our reluctance to risk. So we hold in all our feelings again, and the cycle continues. Yet to heal our hurt self we have to share it with others. So where do we start?

Rather than hold it in and then let it out impulsively or haphazardly, we can begin one step at a time. Find someone who we know is safe and supportive, such as a trusted friend, a counselor or therapist, a therapy group, self help group or a sponsor. Begin by risking one little thing. Follow the share-check-share guideline. [40] If it works, share some more. Risking and sharing involves several other core issues, including trust, control, feelings, fear of abandonment, all-or-none thinking and behaving, and high tolerance for inappropriate behavior. When any of these issues come up, it can be useful to consider, and even to begin talking about it with safe people. As we risk, we can eventually begin to tell our story.

TELLING OUR STORY

Telling our story is a powerful act in discovering and healing. It is a foundation of recovery in self-help groups, group therapy and individual psychotherapy and counseling. Each of our stories when complete contains three basic parts: *separation*, *initiation* and *return*.[21,22] Twelve-Step self help groups describe their stories as "*What we were like*,""*What happened*" and "*What we are like now*" (Figure 9.1 in Chapter 9). People in individual and group therapy may further describe telling our story as risking, sharing, participating and "working" in group. Psychoanalysts may call it "free association, working through transference and through unsolved internal conflict." Among close friends, we may call it "baring our souls" or "having a heart-to-heart talk."

In sharing and telling our story we can be aware that gossip and wallowing in our pain are usually counterproductive to healing. This is in part because gossip tends to be attacking rather than self-disclosing and it is generally incomplete, following the victim stance or cycle (Figure 15 two pages below). Wallowing in our pain is continuing to express our suffering beyond a reasonable duration for healthy grieving. There is a danger here that that may happen in some self-help meetings: When a person tries to tell a painful story that has no apparent or immediate resolution, the other members may unknowingly label it as "self-pity" or a "pity party." In this case, while self-help meetings are generally safe and supportive, if that happens, the bereaved may wish to look elsewhere to express their pain.

In 1979 grief researcher and expert Bertha Simos said, "Grief work must be shared. In sharing, however, there must be no impatience, censure [from others] or boredom with the repetition, because repetition is *necessary* for *catharsis* and internalization and eventual unconscious acceptance of the reality of the loss. The bereaved are sensitive to the feelings of others and will not only refrain from revealing feelings to those they consider unequal to the burden of sharing the grief, but may even try to comfort the helpers" (i.e., the listener). [80b]

Our story does not have to be long. In telling our story we talk about what is important, meaningful, confusing, conflicting or painful in our life (i.e., more core issues). As we talk we risk, share, describe, interact, explore, discover and more. And by so doing we heal our painful trauma effects. While we listen to the stories of others, and they listen to ours, perhaps the most healing feature is that *we*, the story teller, get to *hear our own story* as we tell it. While we may have an *idea* about what our story is when we *start* to tell it, it usually comes out different from what we initially thought —an advantage to our being real as we talk.

I have illustrated an overview of important parts of our story in Figure 16. Starting at the point on the circle called "contentment," we can forget that we are in our story. Eventually in our day-to-day life we experience a loss, whether it be a real or a threatened loss. The stage is now set for both grieving *and* growing. In the figure, I have summarized most of the initial pain of our grieving as hurt. And when we feel hurt, we tend to get sad, fearful, angry, and often frustrated.

FIGURE 16. OUR STORY EXPANDED, INCLUDING MARTYR/VICTIM cycle [104]

At this crucial point we have a possibility of becoming more aware that we have experienced a loss or are suffering a past or current trauma. And here we can choose to make a commitment to facing our emotional pain and grieving head-on. If we remain aware and *work through* our pain, we can call this cycle of our story the "hero/heroine's journey" (see also Fig 9.1 on page 51). *Or* we may remain *un*aware of the possibility of working through our pain around our loss or upset. We may then begin to build up a resentment and/or to blame ourselves, which eventually leads to stress-related illness, and to more prolonged suffering than if we had worked through our upset and our grieving in the first place. We can call this even more-painful-in-the-long-run cycle the "*victim cycle*" or the "*martyr/victim stance.*"

We tell our story from and as our Real Self to safe people by being honest about the details of what our life has been like for us over time *and* right now —and our feelings about it all. In their book *The Spirituality of Imperfection*, Ernie Kurtz and Katherine Ketcham elaborate on the power of storytelling in AA from many angles, including the inevitability of emotional pain. They suggest that trying to be perfect both in and outside of telling our story may be our most tragic human mistake. Perfectionism is a burden. They say that spirituality is not avoiding errors or their consequences, but rather learning how to *live with* them. As *A Course in Miracles* describes, to grow it is not useful to beat ourselves up for making a mistake. Instead, we can share the pain of our mistakes by telling our story to safe others.

If we commit to work through our pain and grieving, we then begin to share, express, participate and to experience our grief. We may need to tell our story in such a fashion several times periodically over a period of several hours, days, weeks or even months—in order to finally complete it. We may also have to consider it in other ways, mull it over, dream about it and tell it yet again and again.

While doing so has been painful for us, if we share we will eventually be complete with our upset or conflict. We will be free of its pain. Our conflict is now eventually resolved and integrated. We learn from it. By so being real, we regain our Real Self and grow. And we settle back to our natural state, which is peace, joy and creativity.

However, to begin to tell our story may be difficult. And when we tell it, it may be difficult to express our real feelings around it. Among our most difficult feelings to recognize and to express is anger. Anger is a major component in grieving and in healing our Child Within, which I address next.

GETTING ANGRY

Anger is one of the most common and important of our feelings. Like other feelings it is an indicator of what we might need to attend to. People who grew up in a troubled family and world often do not realize how angry they are. They may not know how useful it can be for them to recognize and express their anger healthily—even if their traumas happened long ago. When they were young, they were often repeatedly mistreated, which may have been subtle. Children and adults often don't realize that they have been mistreated. Having no other reference point from which to test reality, they think that they were treated—and often still being treated—is somehow appropriate or OK. Or if not appropriate, they somehow *deserved* to have been mistreated.

Through hearing the stories of others in recovery, we slowly learn what mistreatment, abuse or neglect actually is. In recovery in group therapy, individual therapy, or Twelve Step fellowship groups, becoming and being aware of our feelings and expressing them is a distinct advantage in eventually living a successful and peaceful life. As we discover our hurts, losses and traumas we can begin the necessary and freeing process of grieving. Becoming aware of our anger and expressing it is a major part of that grieving process.

One of the few deficiencies of some members in some Twelve Step self-help groups is their hidden fear of feelings and emotions, especially painful ones. There is even a saying "H.A.L.T.S."—don't get too hungry, angry, lonely, tired or serious. The newly recovering person can just as easily take this to mean "hold in your feelings" over its more accurate meaning "take better care of yourself so that you can help prevent being overwhelmed by these feelings."

Many people in recovery are afraid to express their anger. They are often fearful that they might lose control if they really got angry. Then they might hurt someone, hurt themself or something else bad might happen. Were they to pursue it, they would often discover that their anger is not a superficial upset, but is actually rage. And to be enraged is scary. It is normal to be scared over becoming aware of and fully expressing our anger.

Often accompanying being angry, there may be somatic or nervous symptoms, such as trembling, shaking, panic, loss of appetite and at times even a feeling of excitement. Sometimes it can be freeing to get in touch with and express our anger. Yet in a troubled family or environment, the healthy awareness and expression of feelings is often discouraged and may even be forbidden.

In an environment where feelings can't be expressed, we may feel as though *we* caused the loss or trauma. We feel shame and guilt. But it may not be OK to openly express these either. So we may then feel even more angry, and if we try to express *that*, we are squelched again. With repeated stuffing or repressing of such feelings, our Child Within is left feeling confused, sad, shameful and empty. As these painful feelings build and accumulate, they begin to become intolerable. With nowhere to ventilate them, our only choice seems to be to block them all out as best we can—to become numb.

We actually have four additional choices, which we may learn as we grow older: 1) to hold it in until it gets unbearable; 2) unable to let it out, we get physically or emotionally sick, and/or we may "blow up;" 3) to blot the pain out with alcohol, other drugs or other addictions; or the most likely to succeed—4) to express the anger and work it through with safe and supportive people.

Blotting anger out with alcohol or other drugs, whether prescribed by a physician or self-administered, is generally not effective for long and may be dangerous. A problem is that many of us have reached out for help and have been given drugs rather than be shown that we are grieving and encouraged to work through it.

PROTECTING OUR PARENTS: A BLOCK TO GRIEVING

Earlier I listed six ways that we may use to avoid the pain of grieving: denying our loss, intellectualizing about it, stuffing our feelings, being macho, using alcohol or drugs and prolonged attempting to get the lost object back.

In further discussing anger we can now describe another block to grieving: that of protecting our parents and other parent and authority figures from our anger. We may sense, believe or fear that if we get angry at our parents or parent figures, it will not be appropriate or that something bad will happen. Below I list nine ways that we tend to protect our parents from our anger.

The first way is by outright denial. We may say something, like, "Oh, my childhood was fine" or "I had a normal childhood." Such was their trauma, that many adult children of alcoholic, troubled or dysfunctional families cannot remember 75% or more of their childhood experiences. In my clinical experience, however, when working in recovery, most adult children *are* able to work through the denial and to gradually uncover their ungrieved hurts, losses or traumas and work through them. Hearing others' stories in group therapy, ACA or CoDA self-help meetings and elsewhere is a help in identifying and recognizing what happened to us. We can then begin to mobilize our grieving, which includes getting angry.

The second approach to protect our parents is by taking an appeasing attitude, such as "Yes, my childhood may have been somewhat bad, but my parents did the best they could." Doing so is often a way that we detach from our feelings, assuming that such a "why bother"

Table 16.1. Answers, Approaches and Strategies often Used to Protect the Parents (and thus Block Healing)

Category	*Frequently Heard*

1) **Outright denial**   "My childhood was fine"

2) **Appeasing** "Yes, but . . ." detaching from the feelings "It happened but . . . they (my parents) did their best"

3) **Viewing pain of the trauma as a *fantasy*** "It really didn't happen that way."

4) **Fourth Commandment** (Catholic) or **Fifth** (Protestant & Hebrew) "God will be angry at me for any of my anger at my parent(s)"

5) **Unconscious fear of rejection**   "If I express my anger or rage, they won't love me"

6) **Fear of the unknown**   "Something really bad will happen. I might hurt someone, or they might hurt me"

7) **Accepting the blame**   "I'm the bad one"

8) **Forgiving the parents** "I'll just forgive them" or "I've already forgiven them"

9) **Attacking the person who suggests doing recovery work** "You're bad for suggesting that I express my hurt and rage or that my parents could have abuse me."

---

stance   prevents us from beginning necessary grief work in getting free of our suffering.

Next is viewing the pain of our loss or trauma as being a fantasy. This one is commonly projected onto us if we do our recovery work in psychoanalysis or some psychoanalytically oriented psychotherapy. The analyst or therapist may suggest or imply that if a trauma happened to us, we never can remember it the way that it actually happened, with the implication that it is a fantasy. Compounding the wound, this once again invalidates the pain of our Child Within. [68] We end up concluding something like, "It really didn't happen that way." Another most and closely related defense is the claimed "false memory syndrome" which was made up by an organized group of parents who were accused by their now adult children of molesting them. Since their inception in 1992, there has been no definitive data-based study that verifies any such entity as "fms." [95, 96]

Some tell us that while we may hate our parents, we also love them, and that what they did wrong was only out of love. Alice Miller (1981) says, "The adult patient knows all this, but he is glad to hear it again because it helps him once more to deny, pacify and control the Child Within him who has just begun to cry. In this way, the therapist or the group, or he himself, will talk the child out of his 'silly' feelings because they are no longer appropriate in the present situation (although still intense); a process that could have produced positive results—namely, the awakening and maturation of the child's true self—will be undermined by a method of treatment that refuses to offer support to the angry child." To get free from mistreatment, we usually first need to get angry *and then* grieve our traumas.

The next way of blocking our anger is by the Fourth Commandment (or Fifth—if Protestant & Hebrew), which says "Honor thy father and thy mother, that their days may be long upon the land which the Lord thy God giveth thee." (King James Version, Exodus 20:12). It is difficult to decipher or interpret exactly what the word "honor" means in this context. Over the centuries, however, it has been interpreted by most parents to mean "no back talk" and other such stifling messages to the child. We may conclude from this Fourth Commandment something like, "God will be angry at me if I get angry at my parents. It just isn't right," or "I will be an evil or a bad person if I get angry at them." Most organized religions around the world have similar exhortations, which tend to stifle our true self and our ability to be real and work through our losses in a healthy way.

A fifth way of avoiding our anger and grieving by protecting our parents is by being afraid of them rejecting us. We may consider, think or say something like, "If I express my rage, they won't love me," or "They may treat me like a bad little boy or girl again." This is a genuine fear that needs to be expressed when it comes into our awareness.

A sixth way is by being fearful of the unknown, or being afraid of expressing feelings. We may say or think, "Something really bad will happen. I might hurt someone or they might hurt me." This is another genuine fear that we may need to express in recovery. We may also accept the blame onto ourself, saying, "I'm the bad one."

Many people avoid their anger and their grief by simply "forgiving" their parents of their abuse. Assuming that forgiving is an easy act, they may say "I'll just forgive them." Or often more stifling to their True Self, "I've *already* forgiven them." However, most people who say this have not forgiven completely, since forgiving is a process that is analogous to, if not in large part identical to the grieving process.

A final method of protecting our parents is by attacking the person who suggests that we may need to do recovery work, especially any work that might involve expressing anger at our parents. We may say or think something like, "You are bad for suggesting such a thing!" or "How dare you suggest that my parents could have been inadequate or bad?"

In one or in a combination of these ways, we protect our parents from our hurt, anger and rage. And by doing so, we stifle our True Self and block our ability to recover from needless suffering. However, we are now armed with the knowledge of the possibilities of these blocks. Now, when we start to use these excuses in any way—perhaps unknowingly, to impede our grieving—we can begin to let go of them when we are ready.

HELPING EXPRESS OUR ANGER

We're learning that in healing it is appropriate and healthy to become aware of and to express our anger safely. But how can we express it? And to whom? It is becoming clearer to us that there are some people who are able to listen to our anger and to help us process it. These are the safe and supportive people that I have mentioned—therapists, counselors, sponsors, therapy groups and self-help group members and safe trusted friends. By contrast, there are other people who, for one reason or another, are unable to tolerate or to hear our anger. These may include our parents and others who may in some way remind us of our parents.

If we express ourself the way we need to, directly to the parent or other person in question, it is unlikely that we can complete a healing experience. They may well not understand what we are trying to say or what we are trying to do. Or they may reject our expression, our risk sharing, and we may feel confused, hurt and powerless again. While it would be cathartic if we could ventilate our anger to our abusers in a healthy way, doing so would likely not be in our best interest. And it might even end up being self-destructive. Because they have not healed *their own* hurt Real Self, they are generally unable to be a part of the safe and supportive process of another's healing. However, we can learn to set limits so that they do not continue to mistreat us. We set limits with both firmness and love. We do so not with aggressiveness, but with assertiveness.

While it is usually helpful to eventually make peace with and, through the grieving and letting-go process, to forgive our parents and others who have mistreated us, it is important that we not rush this process. There are some therapists and counselors who may insist on making reconciliation with our parents an immediate or ultimate goal of therapy. But premature efforts in this direction can actually block discovering and healing. It is usually best to take our time.

And even if we work for a long time to discover and heal our Real Self, we may not be able to heal our differences with our parents. We come to the realization that we cannot fix them. They are the way they are, and nothing that we can do will change that. And so we let go. Letting go may be a more realistic term than forgiving.

Wisdom to Know The Difference

For some people whose parents or others—such as an actively alcoholic, violent or otherwise abusing person—are "toxic" to them, it may be helpful to separate from them for a few months to a year, or more. Such a separation or "detoxification" period provides a space and a peace that will allow us to begin to begin to heal.

The more we were hurt by the lost object or event that we grieve, the more anger we generally have stored. And even if we had a fairly healthy relationship with the lost one, we can still get angry at it for leaving us helpless and deprived. We may also get angry at others, including those we believe in some way were responsible for our loss, and sometimes at anyone not suffering as we are. Finally, we may get angry at having to pay for counseling and even at our counselors or therapists for pushing us to do our grief work. All of this is grist for the mill of our recovery work.

The answer is to get real, share our hurt with safe others, grieve over time, and then let go of our accumulated pain. We finally let our anger and resentments go. Then we can use any new anger *efficiently* as an assistant and motivator to get back to an emotional and behavioral equilibrium and a successful life.

17   DIFFICULTY TRUSTING

Trust is a major factor and dynamic throughout our life. It is needed for healthy exchanges in *nearly every* relationship, interaction and profession. Without trust, relationships tend not to work well. Barbara Misztal says that real trust offers several advantages: 1) It makes it easier for people to live and work together, 2) it makes our social life more predictable, and 3) it creates a sense of community.

Trust is the willingness of we (the trustor) to be vulnerable to the actions of another (the trustee or trusted one), with a reasonable expectation or confidence that they will behave in an appropriate or beneficial way to us. Of course there is risk of harm to us if they don't behave accordingly. Commonly if the trustor has low to no control or enforcement over the trustee's aggressive or hurtful actions and yet continues to trust them, it can result in enabling behavior and high tolerance for inappropriate behavior.

Trust usually evolves from our one-on-one experiences. Trust is earned: before we offer or extend our trust, the other must prove trustworthy by showing qualities that promote trust (Table 17.1). Otherwise we distrust or at best rely on faith or hope. A problem is that *as children* we may have wanted to trust our parents and others, but when they did any of the actions in the left column of Table 17.1 we were mostly helpless to stop them. Many of us have trusted and been betrayed by our parents, other family members, authority figures and other relationships so much that it can be hard for us to trust another who gets close to us.

TABLE 17.1 QUALITIES PROMOTING TRUST V. DISTRUST

Promote *Distrust* (In parents & other relationships)	Promote *Trust* (In healthy parents & other healthy relationships)
Repeated inappropriate behavior	Consistent appropriate behavior
Does not do what says will do	Does what says will do
Breaks agreements & promises	Keeps agreements & promises
Abusive &/or neglecting	Neither abusive nor neglectful
Tries to control me	Lets me be me
Dynamics and Results	
Unhealthy development (from *dis*trust-promoting factors above) leads to ...	Healthy development in a healthy family and world results in ...
... a sense of insecurity and mistrust	... security, trust, and optimism
Occurs in: 80% of families	20% of families

Mistrust v. Distrust: *Mis*trust is suspecting or believing that another has a hidden agenda. *Dis*trust is a lack or absence of trust that may use the saying "Trust, but verify" and can appropriately lessen some untrustworthy people's power over us. Since it is likely that I was wounded by my family and society of origin—where mistreatment probably started at an early age and was inconsistent and unpredictable—how can I ever learn to trust? If these are the kinds of relationships that I have grown up with, how can I know any differently? So I will probably find current and future relationships with similar unhealthy qualities, where I will be repeatedly mistreated, and all of which will enforce my difficulty trusting.

Trust is believing that the trusted person will do what they say they will or what is expected. It starts in the family and grows or lessens with our relationships with others. Erikson said that development of basic trust is the first psychosocial developmental state occurring, or failing to, during the first two years of life. Healthy development in a healthy family and world results in a prolonged sense of security, trust, and optimism, while failure (from *dis*trust-promoting factors in the left column of Table 16.1) leads to a sense of insecurity and mistrust. My estimate is that this kind of healthy development occurs in up to 20% of families, which explains why difficulty trusting is a core issue for so many of us in the 80% majority.

Karen was a 40-year-old adult child of a dysfunctional family. While she often felt loved by her father, he and her mother repeatedly teased and rejected her. It took her over a year to trust her therapy group enough for her to tell them of her having been repeatedly mistreated as a child, including having been sexually abused by her father. She also spoke of flip-flopping between overly trusting (often too loose boundaries) and not trusting at all (rigid boundaries). By risking to share her Real Self and her inner life, including her painful memories, with the group and other safe people, she has slowly learned to trust in a healthier way.

Trust is one of the most basic of the core issues because it is intimately linked with nearly all the other core and other issues and is crucial for nearly all of our relationships.

• If I can't trust you in the most important interfaces of our lives, how can we have a close relationship?
• If I can't know and trust myself and most of my inner life, how can I know if and when you—or someone else—may be mistreating me?
• How then can I set healthy boundaries to prevent abuse or neglect?

Part of trusting is *feeling safe.* Unless I feel safe with you and with others, I cannot trust you by sharing my True Self with you.
• If I go to a helping professional or an authority figure for help, can I trust baring my soul to them?
• If it is too scary for me to be real with anyone, then how can I even get to know my Real Self?

Healthy boundaries are important in recovery and in life because they let my True Self come out, in part by protecting its integrity and well-being. In all of these ways and more, healthy boundaries are an important part of trusting (Figure 17.1).

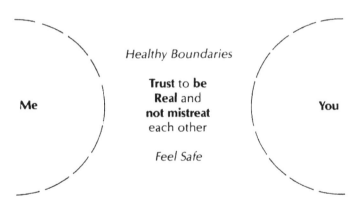

Figure 17.1 Boundaries and Trust

Some brain researchers have traced aspects of trust to the brain's amygdala and caudate nucleus and found that the presence of the hormone oxytocin increases trust.

Lack of ability: How much we trust another is a measure of our belief in their honesty, fairness, or benevolence. The term "confidence" may apply when we believe in the in the other's ability to do what they say they will do. We may forgive a betrayal of trust more easily if it is interpreted as a failure of ability or competence rather than a lack of honesty or integrity.

Other core issues often interacting with trust are: all-or-none, control, difficulty handling conflict, feelings, dependence and fear of abandonment, plus related ideas such as confidence, risk, power and meaning. For example, with all-or-none interacting with difficulty trusting, we may meet a stranger and tell them "all" without their having first earned our trust, only to have them use it against us later. Or as a patient told me, "I trusted a stranger drug dealer who I paid cash in a bad neighborhood to sell me an unknown substance, but wouldn't trust my therapist and wife to tell them about my real pain and drug dependence." Another's breaking our trust can generate conflicts that we may not handle well, such as when we lend them our money and they won't pay us back.

STAGES OF TRUSTING – PART 1

Relationship therapist and author Riki Robbins describes four generic stages of trust, which I summarize in Table 17.2. She gives an example. "When Cathy, a college professor, was betrayed, she experienced total mistrust at first. She asked me, 'Can I trust anyone: myself, other people, or even God?' I asked her if she remembered feeling this way before. She replied, 'Yes. When I was a little girl. My father was a minister devoted to spreading the word of God. Yet he beat me and my brother regularly. It seemed so crazy to me. How could someone who was supposed to be so good act so bad? If I couldn't trust him to back up his words with actions, then I couldn't trust anyone else.' " Her father had betrayed her basic perfect trust.

Many of us were repeatedly traumatized in varying degrees from childhood, often leading to our distrusting others—especially if they remind us of our abusers in any way. Our Real Self, our Child Within went into hiding (Figure 1.1 on page 3), and now we are reminded. *Naming what happened* and *sharing* it with *safe* people and *grieving* our trauma effects can begin slowly to restore our trust with others.

TABLE 17.2. FOUR STAGES OF TRUST
(expanded from Robbins)

Stage of Trust	Description & Comments
Perfect	We are born with perfect trust. But trauma, esp. betrayal trauma,* can erode it from childhood experiences.
Damaged	Someone betrays our trust in them.
Devastated	Happens after a larger betrayal, when you've been repeatedly abused, neglected, lied to, cheated on & treated with disrespect.
Restored	Once damaged or destroyed, it's possible, but difficult; usually takes months to years of recovery work.

*Psychologist Jennifer Freyd: betrayal trauma is abuse and neglect from parents and other caregivers. [35]

CREATING TRUST

Trusting is a choice. While there is no guarantee that we won't be betrayed, as adults we have the power to create trusting relationships. When we meet someone, we can begin to nurture trust by knowing ourself: we can get in touch with our healthy needs, feelings and goals so we can use these to make our life go better, know who we are and what we want from a relationship. If we are honest with ourself, we will be honest with other people. If we tell others the truth, they will tend to reciprocate. If they don't, we can learn that they are not ready or able to share their Real Self, so we can draw back on our sharing.

Find a trustworthy person (who will have one or more of characteristics in the right column of Table 17.1). Practice the recovery admonition: Share, check, share. Watch and listen carefully. If you see signs that they may be unsafe (see Table 5.2 on page 39) or even dangerous (lies, broken promises), heed them. An unsafe or untrustworthy person isn't going to change overnight —even with your good influence.

We can remember another pearl of wisdom: we can look at every difficult, unpleasant or painful relationship event as a learning experience. In so doing, we can come to view such relationship difficulties as *practice* for future relationships instead of all-or-none wherein we tell them either all or nothing about us.

Create trust moment by moment. Whenever a situation surfaces where we sense that our trust is being violated by a previously safe person, we can talk about it. It may make both uncomfortable in the short run, but it will likely bring you closer together in the long run. Relationship expert Riki Robbins suggests that if you have serious concerns, ask them: "Where were you yesterday evening when I called and got no answer?" "Why were you two hours late for our meeting today?" If you sense there's something wrong, you may be right. Always follow your observations and interests.

To create trust we need to name and share our feelings—both the painful and the joyful. I can share the truth about who I am, what's going on for me now, and my intentions for the future. When I notice something that's bothering me I can honestly report it. I can resist the temptation to lie at all costs. Lying kills trust, similar to how shaming and threatening another kills their sexual attraction and desire.

For some untrusting but committed couples, when appropriate, Robbins wrote: "Someone posed this question: 'If I tell you the truth—that I lied to you—can you still trust me?' Robbins says that clearly the answer is 'yes'. The secret of creating trust right from the beginning is to have a conversation that goes something like this, 'I have betrayed other people. I may betray you sometimes and you will probably betray me. We will try to avoid it, but when it happens we will deal with it together.' "

Workplace Trust: In the workplace being able to trust one another usually has a positive influence on our behaviors, perceptions, and output. *Structure* and *integrity* set up by the owner tends to promote trust that encourages us to feel comfortable there and to excel. By having a conveniently organized area to work, our concentration and effort will usually increase. Structure increases trust and thereby makes a workplace manageable. People work together and achieve success through trust while working on projects that rely on each person's contribution. (See also page 288)

Trusting drugs: Twelve Step lore warns us of over attachment to people, places and things. Sometimes we may not trust things. When a physician prescribes a drug, can we trust it to do what they and the drug maker claim it will do for us? What has been your experience? Have the drugs worked well? I have learned to be careful of personally taking or prescribing most medical drugs. A classic and key principle to consider is the risk/benefit ratio. The lower that ratio is, the safer and usually more effective it will be. Most antibiotics, hormones, and the like tend to have a low R/B ratio. But psychiatric drugs have such a high R/B ratio that since the 1980s I have distrusted nearly all of them, which psychiatrists Peter Breggin, Joanna Moncrieff, Grace Jackson, others and I have documented. [9,50,51,70,88,103] Psychiatric drugs cause more toxicity, disability and death than all other kinds of prescribed drugs. [9,51,88]

Jim said, "I am a 'social phobic' who has come to realize my problem isn't chemical, it's experiential. I have been betrayed countless times and because of these abusive childhood experiences, until someone earns my trust, I cannot trust them. Doctors gave me drugs for what they labeled me with as 'social phobia,' which made me worse. Fearing rejection, assault or unjust incarceration, I stay home, avoiding work and human interaction; so far this has been my life-long solution to a complete lack of trust in anyone. My solution has been to take people as individuals rather than erroneously thinking that one person's behavior towards me is indicative of "everyone's" opinion. And perhaps not to expect much from people and to protect myself by concentrating on what I want, as long as I'm not harming anyone. I hope I can learn how to trust a few people and find a job to take responsibility for my expenses." Already Jim is more aware of his past and present situation than most people who become disabled from trauma and the psychiatric drugs that make them worse.

PART 2 - SPIRITUAL ASPECTS OF TRUST

Spirituality is about our relationships with our self, others and the God of our understanding. It is about making meaning as we live our life here on Earth and explore the Divine Mystery. The modern spiritual text *A Course in Miracles* shows an expanded view of the stages of trust. The Course says that trust is a main God-given characteristic of each of us as students and teachers of God. In the shortest of its three volumes called the *Manual for Teachers*, the Course devotes seven pages to describing the characteristics of God's teachers. They include being able to trust, be honest, tolerant, gentle, defenseless, generous, patient, faithful, and to feel joy. I summarize the stages in the further spiritual development of trust in Table 17.3. Take a minute or two and read over this table.

These stages are appropriately similar to the process of working the Twelve Steps, as are many other teachings of the Course. Learning to tolerate emotional pain and continuing recovery work, spiritual practice and conscious co-creation with God will help us as we slowly traverse these stages of spiritual trust. For me to understand the powerful psychological and spiritual teachings of the Course I have had to study it regularly for years, which I have summarized in my books *Choosing God* and *Teachers of God*. [101,102]

These above ten characteristics of God's teachers *flow from one another* and—as are the core issues—*inter-related* in other ways. For example, being *honest* flows from being able to *trust*, since we feel safe enough to be our real self with trusted others and God. Another example is that *joy* comes from being *gentle* and *defenseless*. Woven into the fabric of many of these, but not among the list of ten, is the spiritual strength of letting go of judging others.

TABLE 17.3. STAGES IN THE FURTHER SPIRITUAL DEVELOPMENT OF TRUST (FROM *A COURSE IN MIRACLES*)

Stage	Description	Comment
Undoing	Experiencing losses of things & relationships.	Losses and hurts are a normal part of life, not yet knowing the meaning for each.
Sorting out	We begin to sort out which relationships are more meaningful.	All experiences are real only as they are helpful in sorting out what is valuable to us.
Period of relinquish-ment	– of the valueless. Turning the curse into the gift.	Here we sacrifice our own best interests on behalf of [spiritual] truth.
Settling down	We give up what we don't want & keep what we do want.	We rest awhile with God, God's love (Holy spirit) & Christ consciousness.
Period of unsettling	More struggle & sorting out which relationships are more meaningful.	Continued spiritual practice & co-creation with God.
Achievement	After letting go, a period of real peace	Heaven on Earth

Being *non-judgmental* is a way to experience peace, which is a major goal of the Course, which says, "You have no idea of the tremendous release and deep peace that comes from meeting yourself and your brothers totally without judgment. ...judging... in any way is without meaning."

Our trust interacts with our dependence *to* and *upon* others, and specifically that we become relationship-dependent to varying degrees upon our trusted relationships. We can eventually see trust as a better way to resolve such a dependence, being more advantageous in the long term than trying to control them. Trust is valuable if the other is more powerful than us, and yet we may be obligated to support them. I address healthy and unhealthy dependence on others in the next chapter.

18   DEPENDENCE

Throughout our lives we are all dependent on at least a few others in one way or another. Ideally, it is usually a healthy kind of dependence. But it becomes a core issue when we find ourself involved in an *un*healthy kind of dependence. In the table below I show an introductory and simplified view of some of the basic dimensions of this common core issue. Take a minute and study the table. Notice how these five characteristics in the first column define their differences along the spectrum of dependence and independence.

We can become dependent on people, places and things. Healthy dependence is when we can rely on another to support us in any of a number of ways. Dependence has several aspects that involve independence and personal boundaries, as shown in the table.

If I can trust you, then that will help my chances of having a healthy dependent relationship with you. But even if I can't trust you, I still may need to be dependent on you in one or more ways, e.g., for finances and companionship. If I feel unable or unwilling to

Figure 18.1 SPECTRUM OF HEALTHY VS. UNHEALTHY DEPENDENCE / INDEPENDENCE

Characteristic	Unhealthy Independence	Healthy Independence	Healthy Dependence	Unhealthy Dependence
Description of State	Separated, Isolated, Alienated	— Healthy Independence & Dependence —		Victim or martyr, often an enabler
Live from	false self/ego	— True self —		false self/ego
Co-dependent	Yes	— No —		Yes
Boundaries	Inappropriately rigid, disengaged	Appropriate distance & privacy	Appropriate closeness & sharing	Fused & enmeshed
Other Core Issues involved	Common, from trust to difficulty handling conflict	Other core issues may be involved at times.		Common, from trust to difficulty handling conflict

leave our relationship, I can use healthy boundaries to protect myself from being mistreated or abused. But if I am a little child, totally dependent upon troubled, distracted or even toxic parents or parent figures, how can I survive unless I let down my awareness and boundaries and try to trust my parents? And so, through a series of traumas, I may end up experiencing and learning unhealthy boundaries, unhealthy dependence and independence, as well as difficulty trusting.

A self-actualized or recovered person has a balance of healthy dependence among their relationships *and* healthy *in*dependence both within and outside of them. In healthy dependence there is appropriate closeness and sharing, and in healthy independence there is appropriate distance and privacy (**bold** text in Figure 18.1). They have healthy boundaries.

By contrast, the person with unhealthy dependence on others has boundaries that are too loose or diffused, and are enmeshed or fused in their relationships. They may feel like a martyr or a victim and may also be an enabler. A person who is unhealthily independent usually has inappropriately rigid boundaries and tends to be disengaged in many relationships. They often feel separated, isolated and alienated. Both tend to live from being attached to their false self and usually show manifestations of active co-dependence.

WHAT IS HEALTHY DEPENDENCE?

The hyphen in the word co-dependence emphasizes that it is about being in relationships. The ability to be dependent and independent in a healthy way is an important goal in recovery from co-dependence and in most difficult relationships.

Healthy relationships have as crucial components healthy dependence and independence. We cannot have a successful and enjoyable life without being dependent and vulnerable with selected safe people and, if we choose, with our Higher Power.

DEVELOPMENTAL ASPECTS

In the 1940s the Scottish physician and relationships-analyst Ronald Fairbairn emphasized that the evolution of healthy dependence was crucial in healthy child development. He described three stages in this process: 1) our earliest dependence, where as an infant we are so dependent upon and identified with our mother (or other parent figure) that we have little sense that we are a separate person. Then at about 5 to 6-months-old we enter 2) a transitional period, wherein we begin to deal with and adjust to separations from our mother and changes in our relationship. This phase eventually—beginning at about 18 months—includes what psychoanalyst Margaret Mahler called the *rapprochement* stage. The final stage is 3) mature dependence, which develops slowly as a child and as we grow older. Here we learn to accept differences, handle our conflicts and frustrations, and learn about exchange and mutuality.

Ideally, this mature stage develops into healthy *inter*dependence. This mutual dependence interacts with other developmental tasks and core issues such as trust, control and all-or-none thinking and behaving, and can be disrupted by experiencing dysfunctional parenting and other traumas. *In their recovery* trauma survivors usually have to *retrace some of these stages in a safe setting* with healthy parent figures and healthy others. These people may include individual and group therapists, sponsors, group members, friends, colleagues and safe others.

HEALTHY VS. UNHEALTHY DEPENDENCE

In recovery the goal is progress, not perfection. It is neither necessary nor possible to reach all of these qualities of healthy dependence and independence overnight.

Figure A.2 on page 306 in the Appendix illustrates some more of the relationships and interactions among the four possible kinds of dependence. Notice that in healthy dependence and independence we are in a harmonious relationship with our self, safe others and, if we choose, our Higher Power. But in the state of *un*healthy dependence and independence, we are usually co-dependent and often in pain.

HEALTHY DEPENDENCE

As you read the following, consider whether you may have had any of these experiences at any time of your life. In healthy dependence we ask for and accept help when needed and appropriate. We feel safe and secure in the relationship. We trust. The relationship is intimate because each person is real. And each has integrity, which the Second of the Twelve Steps calls "sanity." Each person in the relationship is whole. That means we are aware of and caring for ourself on all levels—physical, mental, emotional and spiritual.

A relationship of healthy dependence includes sharing. This relationship is reciprocal and mutual, so each person does an equal amount of sharing. Each supports the other and accepts the other for who they are. The partners share many characteristics and values, including respect for each other. Healthy dependence also means being flexible and having healthy boundaries. [94] The partners are not manipulative—they do not try to get things indirectly from one another. They are direct in asking for their needs and support.

Even though they ask for what they want and need, people in a healthy dependent relationship do not try to control or exploit and are not abusive. Being dependent on each other also means that the partners in this relationship are also healthily independent. While each has a healthy narcissism or self-caring, they are compassionate with each other. And they include appropriate amounts of shared and spontaneous contact and activities.

The recovered person, comfortable being in healthy dependent relationships, tends to avoid intimate relationships with people who repeatedly show unhealthy dependence and independence. Rather, they prefer to be in relationships with people who are comfortable being dependent *and* independent. Finally, the healthy person has an awareness and experience of the spiritual, and a growing and healthy dependent relationship with their Higher Power.

Table 18.2 summarizes each of these characteristics and more and contrasts them with those of unhealthy dependence.

UNHEALTHY DEPENDENCE

By contrast, as shown in the table's right-hand column, those with *un*healthy dependence have difficulty asking for and accepting help. This may be due to a number of factors.

They may have been hurt enough when they reached out, so that they have difficulty trusting. They may try to control, exploit or abuse one another.

TABLE 18.2. CHARACTERISTICS OF HEALTHY & UNHEALTHY DEPENDENCE (CONTINUED NEXT PAGE)

Dependence → Healthy	→ Unhealthy
Asks for and accepts help when appropriate	Difficulty asking for or accepting help
Integrated: integrity realized	Unintegrated
Trusting	Not trusting
Authentic, real (both parties)	Unauthentic
Sharing	Withholding or uneven
Reciprocal	Unidirectional, or both closed
Supportive	Enabling or unsupportive
Accepting	Overaccepting or unaccepting
Equal	Unequal
Flexible	Inflexible
Boundaries clear and flexible	Boundaries blurred, fused and rigid; enmeshment
Non-manipulative. Ask directly for needs & support	Manipulative (indirect attempts at influence or control)
Non-exploitive	Exploitive
Non-controlling	Controlling
Non-abusive	May be abusive
Partners are healthily independent	Co-dependent or unhealthily independent
Self and other-indulgent. Healthy narcissism	Other-indulgent, often with high tolerance for inappropriate behavior
Appropriate amounts of shared and spontaneous contact and activities	Little genuinely shared. Often planned

---

Dependence → Healthy	→ Unhealthy
Compassionate with others	Objective, passionate or numb
Tends to avoid relationship with co-dependents and unhealthy independents.	Often with abusing or other co-dependents. Usually martyr/victim.
Prefers relationships with healthy dependent and independent people.	May feel bored with healthy people.
Free and growing	Imprisoned and stagnating
Includes Higher Power	May exclude Higher Power

Rather than being healthily independent, they are dependent or independent in an unhealthy way. They frequently experience a high tolerance for inappropriate behavior, and are often overindulgent with others. Little is genuinely shared, and when it is, their activities are often planned and not spontaneous.

In the next chapter I will continue describing this core issue by discussing its related co-issue: independence.

19 DEPENDENCE PART 2: INDEPENDENCE

HEALTHY VS. UNHEALTHY INDEPENDENCE

The core issue of dependence includes independence as an important and indispensable dynamic. In fact, a person cannot have a healthy experience of dependence in relationships without also being independent in a healthy way.

When people are independent in an unhealthy way they are codependent. This is because they are still focused on others to their own detriment. They are so focused that—even with safe and appropriate others—they cannot have a healthy dependent relationship. They may be afraid of closeness and intimacy, often because they have been hurt in past close relationships and because in their childhood they never had healthy relationships modeled for them. They have difficulty trusting and their over-focus on others is manifested by their fear and avoidance of close relationships. This may be carried to such an extent that they cannot generally have relationships where they experience both a healthy dependence and independence. As such, their unhealthy independence is a guise of active co-dependence.

HEALTHY INDEPENDENCE

People with healthy independence ask for help when appropriate and accept it, and thereby is dependent in a healthy way. This help or assistance may be with all sorts of things, from the impersonal to the personal in their life, including help getting their healthy human *needs* met. While at other times they are appropriately independent, they are at almost all times real with themself and with safe others. They are trusting of their True Self.

People who have healthy independence have clear and healthy boundaries. They can be either firm or flexible, as needed and appropriate. They tend not to control, manipulate, exploit or abuse others. They have a healthy sense of self, and care for themselves by getting their needs met without hurting others. In this sense they have a healthy narcissism.

Because they are also healthily dependent, they engage in shared and spontaneous contact and activities with others and on physical, mental, emotional and spiritual levels. They are compassionate with themselves and with others. They prefer relationships with healthy people and avoid relationships with active co-dependents and people who are unhealthily independent. They have a loving and constructive relationship with their Higher Power, and are free and growing.

UNHEALTHY INDEPENDENCE

People with unhealthy independence pretend to be in control, independent and *not* in need of help or assistance from others. But underneath this veneer they have the basic feelings and dynamics of any co-dependent person. They may just manifest their co-dependence differently than the stereotyped co-dependent. Certainly, they have difficulty asking for help and accepting it. So they have difficulty being dependent, and often end up feeling isolated and alone.

Not having fully realized their True Self, they are unable to be authentic in relationships. Even when they are in a relationship, they have difficulty trusting. They have thus not fully experienced their whole self's physical, mental, emotional and spiritual dimensions. Rather than extending and sharing themselves, they withhold. They may often deny important aspects of their inner life and are closed to its empowering experiences. They may have difficulty supporting others and may be critical or rejecting. Being so "independent," they often feel "better than" others.

Those with unhealthy independence often tend to have personal boundaries that are too loose, but more often these are rigid. And knowingly or not, they may try to control, manipulate, exploit or even abuse another. They may be "selfish," i.e., show unhealthy narcissism. They may share little with others. Out of touch with their feelings, they may be "objective" and numb.

When they are in relationships, it is often with other co-dependents. Because they have difficulty being dependent with anyone, they may or may not have an ongoing relationship with their Higher Power. If they do, it may not be fulfilling. They frequently end up feeling as though they have lived a life of imprisonment and stagnation. I summarize these characteristics and more in Table 19.1.

WORKING THROUGH UNHEALTHY DEPENDENCE

It is not easy to work through this core issue of dependence. To do so takes great courage, risking, persistence and patience.

A specific recovery plan may include addressing any of the core issues, including dependence. Table 19.2 is an example part of a treatment plan that includes dependence as an issue.

TABLE 19.1. CHARACTERISTICS OF HEALTHY &
UNHEALTHY INDEPENDENCE

Independence → Healthy	→ Unhealthy
Asks for and accepts help when appropriate	Difficulty asking for or accepting help
Independent	Isolated
Real with self and others	Unauthentic when in relationship
Trusts self	Not trusting
Integrated	Unintegrated
Enjoys self	Withholding
Considering	Denying, closed
Available to support or be supported	No support
Accepting; fulfilling own wants and needs	Rejecting, critical
Content in self/Self	Alone, "better than"
Firm or flexible, as needed	Rigid
Boundaries clear and flexible	Boundaries rigid
Non-manipulative	May be manipulative
Non-exploitive	May be exploitive
Non-controlling	May be controlling
Non-abusive	May be abusive
Appropriately self-caring	Self-indulgent only
Healthy narcissism	Unhealthy narcissism
Appropriate amounts of shared and spontaneous contact and activities	Little shared

---

Independence → Healthy	→ Unhealthy
Compassionate with self	Often objective or numb
Tends to avoid relationships with co-dependents & unhealthy independents. Prefers relationship with healthy dependent and independent people.	When in relationship, is often with a co-dependent. Often attacking or abusive. Frequently impulsive & compulsive.
Free and growing	Imprisoned and stagnating
Includes Higher Power	Usually excludes Higher Power

CO-DEPENDENCE

Unhealthy dependence and unhealthy independence are basic components of co-dependence (Figures 18.1 on page 210 and A.2 on page 302). Focusing on others to our detriment, co-dependence is a disease of lost selfhood. It can mimic, be associated with, aggravate and even lead to many of the physical, mental, and emotional conditions that befall us in daily life. But how does understanding its dynamics help us function better?

We become co-dependent when we turn our responsibility for our life and well-being over to our ego/false self and to other people. Co-dependents become so preoccupied with others that they neglect their True Self —who they really are.

TABLE 19.2. TREATMENT PLAN WITH DEPENDENCE AS AN ISSUE

Problem	What I Want to Happen (Goals)	How I Plan To Accomplish That (Objectives)
Difficulty being in a healthy dependent relationship	Be in at least 2 to 3 healthy relationships (e.g., best friend or spouse, therapy group, and sponsor)	Practice these by the following: **1.** Attend group therapy weekly long term.
		2. Risk asking the group for feedback and assistance on a personal issue at least monthly.
		3. Attend a self-help group of my choice at least weekly.
		4. Within three months of starting the self-help group, get a sponsor and communicate weekly.
		Talk to someone else who feels safe at least weekly about my specific issues around dependence

When we focus so much outside of ourselves we lose touch with our *inner life*. Our inner life is a major part of our consciousness. And our consciousness is who we are: our True Self.

ADDICTION TO LOOKING ELSEWHERE

Co-dependence is the most common of all addictions: the addiction to looking elsewhere. We believe that something outside of ourselves (outside of our True Self) can fill our emptiness. The "elsewhere" may be people, places, things, behaviors or experiences that don't bring us authentic and lasting peace. Whatever it is, we may neglect our own selves for it.

This self-neglect alone is no fun long term, so we must get a short-term payoff of some sort for focusing outward. That payoff is usually a reduction in our painful feelings or a temporary increase in joyful feelings. But this feeling or mood alteration depends principally upon something or someone else, and not on our authentic wants and needs.

We learn to be co-dependent from others around us. In this sense it is not only an addiction but a contagious or acquired illness. From birth, we see co-dependent behavior modeled and taught by a seemingly endless string of important people: parents, teachers, siblings, friends, heroes and heroines. Co-dependence is fundamentally about disordered relationships and is reinforced by the media, government, organized religion and the helping professions.

Co-dependence may be present in any one or a combination of the following situations:

1) Persistent stress-related problems or illness,

2) Stress-related illness that is unresponsive or partially responsive to conventional therapy,

3) Relapse of addictions or other disorders,

4) Most medical or psychological conditions and many problems-in-living, including

5) Difficulties in relationship with self, others and our Higher Power.

While it is not the only causal factor for each of these conditions, it can be helpful therapeutically to view co-dependence as a major underlying condition and dynamic in them.

We develop codependence unconsciously and involuntarily. In its primary form, it begins with mistreatment or abuse to a vulnerable and innocent child by its environment, especially its family of origin, and later by its culture or society. It comes about through the process of wounding, which causes the effects of trauma, which I describe elsewhere. [91, 97, 103]

20 OVER RESPONSIBILITY FOR OTHERS

Many of us trauma survivors who grew up in a troubled family and world learned to become overly responsible for others. It was another survival tool that may have worked for us for a while. It gave us the illusion of being in control and often helped us avoid some of our painful feelings. But what seemed to work for us then may not work well now.

Being so over responsible can happen in any of our relationships *anywhere*, from home to school to the work place and from the helping professions to politics. When we rescue others repeatedly to their detriment it stifles their mental, emotional and moral growth.

A 40-year-old patient of mine told me that he always said "Yes" to anyone's requests at work, and doing that was causing him a lot of frustration and wasted his time. By working on himself for two years in group therapy and by taking a course on assertiveness, he has learned to say "No." He has learned to let others do what *they* are responsible for. He learned what he should *not* do or does *not* want to do. Instead of being overly-responsible for others, he now understands that other people may at times be passive, lazy, irresponsible, and act as if they are the world's victim. But *now* they are not his problem.

Being over responsible for others can take up a lot of our time and drain our energy. It also frustrates us when others won't do what they should and it makes us resentful and them lazier.

GUISES OF OVER RESPONSIBILITY

Being over responsible for others can take many guises. I list and define six kinds in Table 20.1: 1) Micromanaging, 2) Rescuing, 3) Active co-dependence, 4) Political correctness taken to the extreme, 5) "Spoon feeding" others who won't learn on their own, and 6) Projective identification, which is a complex relationship dynamic.

Take a few minutes and read over these definitions in Table 20.1.

These are common ways that being over responsible shows up in many relationships. Do any of these remind you of ways that you or others may have interacted?

Being over responsible for others often occurs when other core issues are also active, especially control, all-or-none, dependence,

TABLE 20.1 GUISES OF OVER RESPONSIBILITY FOR OTHERS

Guise	Characteristics
Micro managing	Over controlling, over focus on details, that can sometimes involve bullying. In the workplace it can involve requests for unnecessary and overly detailed reports.
Rescuing	Inappropriately rescuing or bailing out others from their mistakes for which they should be responsible. "Blood-suckers" can take advantage of the vulnerable.
Active co-dependence	The co-dependent focuses on others to their own detriment by being over responsible for them.
Political correctness taken to extreme	Sometimes related to co-dependence, PC can be a form of denial of certain facts about others that, if overlooked, can return to hurt us. Beyond ordinary politeness, PC is excessive minimizing of others' behaviors or threats. Here PC can be related to the core issue of high tolerance for inappropriate behavior and difficulty handling conflict.
"Spoon feeding"	Giving otherwise responsible people ready-made information or opinions in an oversimplified way, depriving them of original learning, thought or experience.
Projective identification	A complex form of *unconsciously* acting out and expressing the feelings and behaviors *for* another for which *they* should be responsible. The other usually denies their feelings and responsibility and manipulates their rescuer into acting and emoting for them.
Fill-in-the-blank	Look at your relationships and name any ways that you or others may be overly responsible for others

shame, the feeling of guilt, difficulty being real, difficulty trusting, neglecting my own needs, high tolerance for inappropriate behavior and difficulty handling conflict. When one or more of these are involved, knowing what to do about being over responsible can be confusing. A way out is to name the issue as being over responsible and to begin to set healthy boundaries and limits with whomever we may be involved.

BEING *HELPFUL* VERSUS BEING *OVER RESPONSIBLE*

Sometimes we can be helpful to another while *not* being over responsible. Some examples of ways to differentiate these include: 1) If we help them once, but not repeatedly, 2) We help someone in an age-appropriate manner, 3) Help a disabled person who cannot otherwise help themself, 4) Express an observation or concern about another's addiction or inappropriate behavior instead of enabling them, and 5) Give constructive feedback instead of trying to manipulate them (Table 20.2).

You may be able to think of other examples of how to differentiate these two ends of the spectrum from 1) normal and appropriate helping to 2) unhealthy and inappropriate "helping."

TABLE 20.2 BEING HELPFUL V. BEING OVER RESPONSIBLE FOR OTHERS

Characteristic	Being Helpful	Being Over Responsible for Others
Time	Helping once	Repeated helping
Special populations	Helping an infant or older child, or any age disabled person	Helping responsible adults often
Alcohol/drug dependent	Expressing concern	Trying to control their use, or other forms of enabling
Feedback	Constructive	Manipulating to control

When we are over-responsible we are usually oblivious to the several downsides of our stance. We may feel invincible, able to take on our job *and* the jobs of others—or running our life *and* others' lives. But this behavior usually leads to our drained energy, increasing frustration and eventually resentment at the other. Those under-responsible may feel shame at being in that position. We may see them as increasingly irresponsible or even pathetic and they may see *us* as increasingly domineering —or neglectful if we stop rescuing or catering to them.

LETTING GO OF THE PAIN OF OVER RESPONSIBILITY

To escape the over responsibility trap we can access and determine 1) *what* we are being over responsible for in one of our personal life *relationships*. And/or 2) with a co-worker on the job —and the grief that either is bringing us. I can begin by asking myself "What boundaries am I not maintaining with the other?" I can then talk with them kindly but clearly about my decision to stop being over-responsible for them.

Roger Martin, dean of the school of management at University of Toronto, describes it well in his book *The Responsibility Trap* wherein he uses a several step approach. This includes: 1) Assess the grief I am experiencing now by my doing the other's work for them *now* and how it will *likely persist* or get *worse* in the future; 2) Reframe what is likely happening as: a) The other is not inherently lazy, b) I am as responsible as they are because I have continually rescued them by being overbearing and not trusting them to do their job; 3) Choose an issue to address with them; 4) Talk with them kindly about how I am going to let them do their job. He gives an example of how to talk with them: "In the past I started doing X when it was actually your job. I share the blame because I kept doing your job without saying anything about it. I'm getting overworked and tired—while you are getting rusty. I want to change that frustrating situation for everyone's sake. I need your help to do that. In the future, will you be willing to do X as we have written in your job description now?"

Then 5) Monitor what happens over time. Correct any missteps along the way. Address any other unaddressed over/under-responsibility issues. 6) Repeat the above steps as needed. This approach can be used in both our personal life and in the workplace. I summarize these actions in Early, Middle, Advanced and Recovered stages below.

Stages of Letting Go of Over-Responsibility

Early	Middle	Advanced	Recovered
Personal Life Identify personal issues and boundaries	Beginning to set personal boundaries	Continuing to set limits	Being responsible for self with clear boundaries
Workplace Evaluate our role and Reframe the other's	Propose a new way for sharing so the other takes responsibility. Use job description.	Practicing a new way of appropriate responsibility for all involved over time	The other takes responsibility for job tasks and does them

21   DIFFICULTY GIVING AND RECEIVING LOVE

This is often the last core issue to be addressed, and for a reason. It is paradoxically both the most difficult and—ultimately after a lot of commitment and attention in a relationship—the easiest—but only after we have done the hard work through most of the other core issues.

The poet songwriter said,

Isn't love strange,
A word we arrange,
With no thought or care,
Maker of despair... [62]

Love is usually the most psychologically and spiritually invigorating of our feelings. Yet, most of us have been hurt over love by disappointment, rejection and betrayal. As a result we often become reluctant to risk expressing our love to anyone. And we may not trust others when they express their love to us. So how can we approach giving and receiving love? What do we know about love?

KINDS OF LOVE

We can sort out seven kinds or levels of love. Going from *bottom to top* in Table 21.1, the most limited kind of love is that which is "ordered" or demanded by an authority figure—such as in a religion or from a master to a servant—and which is not actually love.

Often called being "in love," the next kind is an immature love where the person is overtaken by spontaneous passion that is obsessive, risky, and temporary. [74] For example, Hollywood's ideas of romantic love have twisted all of our ideas about what love is. We may have tried (before recovery) to look for that "special one"—that always seems to pop up in the movies. At first we don't know that this is just entertainment. Becoming attached to the idea that a special other complete us usually brings pain. We can find that love for ourself in our own heart. A companion ideally supports our personal and spiritual growth. But they can't fill us up. That is our job.

Once we find this supportive "other" in our lives, we can make it romantic in a new way. We can learn what their love language is—how they give and receive love—described two pages below. Experiencing real love is more gratifying and fulfilling, and better than anything from Hollywood.

The next two in the table are more real kinds of love that we experience as friend to friend (sometimes called "agape" love) and then parent to child love. Sibling love evolves over time, usually increasing more in adulthood if the relationship is healthy.

Table 21.1   SEVEN LEVELS OF LOVE & THEIR CORE CHARACTERISTICS

Level of Love	Characteristics	Vision/Sight	Level of Consciousness
Highest spiritual (unconditional)	We are love, core of our being and One with God	Visionary, creative, surrender	Unity
Peaceful Being	Humility, "nobody special"	Clear	Compassion
Spouse to spouse, "companionate"	Mature love, grows over time, high commitment & intimacy	Open, secure, supportive comfortable	Understanding, wholeness
Parent for Child	Natural, empathy	Vision of better future	Awakening, Heart
Friend to friend	Spontaneous, grows	"Agape" love	Mutuality
Immature, limerence, "Courtly love," lovesickness	"In-love," "smitten," passionate, spontaneous, obsessive, risky, temporary	Usually blind	Unconscious passion, "chemistry"
Simple religious view Servant to master	By Commandments Not spontaneous	To "Flock" at lower level, teaching of sin and guilt. Blind	Survival, neediness, unconscious

MATURE LOVE

Next in love's evolution is mature love from spouse to spouse. It develops and grows over time, involving high commitment and intimacy. Mature love is open, secure, supportive and comfortable. It is often difficult to achieve, since most couples have many of the unhealed core issues that I address throughout this book (some of which can manifest in adversarial ways, including taking each other's inventory [see section in Appendix on fair fighting] and other forms of argument). Unresolved, these core issues commonly trigger painful conflicts and verbal fights in relationships.

Other factors frequently trigger core issues and resulting conflicts as well, such as different preferences by each partner about how to best: 1) manage money and finances, 2) relate to children and other relatives, 3) decide where to live, 4) communicate with one another, 5) express sexual intimacy, 6) handle recreation and travel, and more.

When we are vulnerable, real, and can share our emotional and physical pain with a safe partner who we can trust not to use what we share with them against us, we will likely grow. Some call this new way of being in relationship as "being on the same side." Martha Beck said, "In real life, two people who are dwelling in Oneness never struggle. They communicate.

They share. They learn to understand one another. They're on the same side, in a game that's played by remaining perpetually aware that all people are One." [7]

When the two each heal themselves over time, work through their conflicts, gain humility and accept each other as they are, their life and their love gets easier, richer and more mature. For most of us who were never shown healthy role models for relationships, this shift from the adversarial coupleship to being on the same side and working together is at first an amazing relief and grows into a kind of love that was worth all the struggle it took to get there. [100]

The next level of love is when we choose love over fear and we exist generally with an attitude of love for all beings and other living things. Knowing that we are "nobody special," we have the aid of humility. Being nobody special is confusing to our ego/intellect. We thought that becoming "somebody special" would answer all of our wishes. But being nobody special releases us from constantly trying to keep our minds busy with how special we are. Here we feel what *A Course in Miracles* calls "complete peace and joy." Most of the time we feel love in our hearts and see others without judgment. We see others as struggling *spiritual beings* who are working at having a *human* experience. We are all on the same path. Some of us are further along than others, but we are all trying to find peace and love.

The poet continued from above:

> Isn't love strange,
> A word we arrange,
> With no thought or care,
> Maker of despair
> *Each breath that we breathe,*
> *With love we must weave,*
> *To make us as one...* [62]

Reading these words on this page won't likely move most unless they have seen and heard them performed by the poet songwriters, which I recommend that you consider viewing. [62]

GIVING LOVE: EXPRESSING LOVE

Gary Chapman wrote about his observations on the "Five Love Languages," helping people speak and understand emotional love when it is expressed directly or indirectly through any one or more of 1) **words of affirmation**, 2) **physical touch**, 3) acts of **service**, 4) **quality time**, and/or 5) receiving **gifts** (Table 21.3). Chapman argues that while each of these languages is enjoyed to some degree by all people, a person will usually speak one primary love language, but all are important and can be ranked after taking the love language profile that is included in his book for both husbands and wives (see below).

TABLE 21.2. THE 5 LOVE LANGUAGES
(summarized from Gary Chapman's work)

Love Language	Examples
Words of affirmation	Using words to affirm the other. 'I'm so proud of you for _____!' , 'You look good in that outfit,' and the like. 'I love you' also usually works.
Physical touch	Touching, holding hands, hugging, kissing.
Acts of service	Doing things for them—from cooking, housework, fixing things —even to getting bugs off of the windshield of their car, they feel loved.
Quality time	Giving them your undivided attention. Looking into their eyes and talking is quality time. So is taking a walk or going out to eat, so long as you are communicating with each other.
Receiving gifts	The gift says, 'He/She was thinking about me. Look what they got for me.'

Out of these five love languages, Chapman believed that everyone has a primary love language. But in my experience *many* of us have *more than one*. Check it out for yourself.

To help determine what your love language(s) may be, go online and take a survey test at www.5lovelanguages.com/assessments/love/. Then show your results to your loved one and ask them to do the same.

From Chapman's observations, whatever makes *us* feel loved is what *we do* or express toward our spouse. For example, when a husband who's main love language is physical touch comes home and goes to the kitchen, he wants his wife to feel loved. He starts hugging her. She says, 'Leave me alone! Can't you see that I am busy?' His problem is not his sincerity. He was sincere. The problem was that he was speaking *his* language and *not her* language. If acts of service is her love language, the best he might do would be to say, 'Honey, why don't you sit down and rest. Let me finish that.' Then she feels loved, since he is speaking her language.

Another example: A wife comes home from work to find her husband almost in tears. He tells her that his boss yelled and threatened to fire him. He is shaking. *Her* love language is words of affirmation —although neither of them understands *yet* what their love language is. She tells him what a good worker he is and how smart he is. His boss doesn't appreciate what a hard worker he is. He becomes more agitated from her words, thinking that if he's so "good," how come he is losing his job? At this point he's about to project his anger at his boss *onto her* because he thinks that she is making him feel worse.

If she understood that *his* love language is physical touch, she could have put her arms around him and held him until his shaking stopped. Then she might have continued to hold him while saying that if he loses his job he will find another one because he is so competent (her main love language, words of affirmation, while filling his needs to be touched). Hearing herself say that calms her down because it is true *and* what *she* also needs to hear.

A third and final example couple are in the same situation, but who are *both aware* of each other's love language. *His* love language is quality time. When he comes home upset and afraid, she could suggest that they go for a walk together. He may need to walk briskly until he settles down and then start to talk it out with her. She's feeling pretty threatened by his boss's words because they can't make it on her salary alone. *Her* love language is words of affirmation. So, once he calms down, he thanks her for getting him outside and walking. *He* can also tell her that he knows they are a great team and somehow they will work this out together if he loses his job. He has gotten his quality time and she has gotten a positive sense of how the two of them are a team (on the same side, "love and honor") and can get through this together. They are both supporting each other through this crisis instead of "using" each other to vent their emotional pain.

These are three examples of the dynamics within this core issue of difficulty giving and receiving love and ways to give and receive love in a healthy way. Using these love language principles shows us how to function as a team instead of attacking one another.

REFRAMING LOVING MY SELF

We can reframe the importance of loving ourself as self interest and self caring.

Before recovery others discouraged loving our self. Some of us believed we were even "rotten to the core!" Throughout recovery we may have fought with our ego/false self often. Credible self help books showed us how to take our life back from our false self. Sometimes it seemed that we were making headway and then we fell victim to what psychologist Bill Tollefson called "the voice of the abuser's values" in our heads telling us all the painful material that we were told in our childhood when we were defenseless and unable to stop all that "junk" from coming in. [85]

As we work through our core issues, we become more adept at dealing with these negative voices. We may realize that "If I can't love myself, I can't love anyone else." What do I need to give up to let love in?

22 BASIC DYNAMICS IN RELATIONSHIPS

In addition to core issues, relationships have 12 dynamics that are basic to their healthy development and functioning. These interaction dynamics usually operate in our relationship with any person, place, thing, behavior or experience.

TABLE 22.1 THE 12 BASIC DYNAMICS IN RELATIONSHIPS

Healthy/Ideal Dynamic	*Opposing* Dynamic
Need or Enjoyment	Addiction or Attachment
Relationship	No Relationship
Bonding	Bondage
Sameness	Differentness *
Spontaneity and Flexibility	Roles, Rituals and Habits*
Mutuality	Pursuing and Distancing, if rigid
Boundaries and Limits	Fusion and Enmeshment
Intimacy or Closeness	Limited Acquaintance & Superficiality
Relationship and Family Health	Family Dysfunction
Healthy Self-Caring / Narcissism	Unhealthy Narcissism
Content	Process *
Growth	Stagnation or Regression

* These are not necessarily unhealthy or undesirable

They often develop and flow from early to later in the following sequence (Table 22.1). Before I begin a relationship, I usually have a *need* for something about that relationship, or I may *enjoy* or gain from it in some way.

NEED OR ENJOYMENT
VS. ADDICTION OR ATTACHMENT

The relationship may either offer or it may actually provide or give me something. Having a healthy openness to what comes up for me in my inner life in that relationship may help my not becoming attached or addicted to the particular person, place or thing. But if at any time during this relationship I do not maintain this healthy openness and balance, I may become addicted, attached or compulsive about the relationship.

Living from and as my real self and having *healthy boundaries* will help me to enjoy and get my needs met in the relationship and will help prevent my becoming addicted or attached to the person, place or thing. While boundaries and limits are sometimes referred to as being an "issue," e.g., a "boundary issue," I find it helpful to describe them more accurately as being a basic dynamic in a relationship. During such a relationship, setting healthy boundaries and limits may be appropriate with anyone, at anytime and anywhere. And letting go of them may also be appropriate, whenever I may choose. I will say more on boundaries later.

RELATIONSHIP VS. NO RELATIONSHIP

Once having experienced getting something that I may want or need in a healthy way, if I want to go further, I can now choose to be in an early stage of what I may like to be a more serious relationship. Or I can just be in the relationship in a limited way, as described in the dynamic of *Intimacy or Closeness* below. Or I can choose not to be in any kind of relationship with this person, place, thing or behavior. Doing so is always my choice, at any time.

BONDING VS. BONDAGE

If I choose to be in that relationship, I may then begin a process of healthy bonding. If I do not maintain healthy boundaries and limits and do not remain attentive to my True Self and its inner life, I could end up in bondage, actively co-dependent and feeling trapped in this relationship, like a martyr or a victim.

By now you may notice that each of these basic dynamics is concerned with being aware of our inner life, with boundaries and with making choices. Each basic dynamic also has a healthy side and an unhealthy side. (In any given relationship it usually takes a while to recognize and sort out what is healthy and unhealthy for us. There may be no need to hurry, so in your recovery give yourself enough time.) It may demonstrate some other form of opposites, which may be further illustrated by the next basic dynamic. In a conventional romantic relationship, this dynamic may also be triggered by "falling in love" (discussed in Chapter 21) or having a sexual affair. But it does not mean real love.

SAMENESS VS. DIFFERENTNESS

As the relationship continues to evolve, I may next encounter the dynamic of sameness and differentness. In my relationship I may notice what things we have in common and how we are different. Either of these can be a plus or a minus, depending on how each sees and handles it. Sameness and differentness are important in my choosing to continue and maintain the relationship —or choosing to end it at any time.

SPONTANEITY AND FLEXIBILITY VS. ROLES, RITUALS AND HABITS

Eventually I may begin to notice that we are each taking on roles and enacting some rituals and habits. For example, when we get together, I may be the one who drives the car, and we may meet every Wednesday night for dinner. This can be healthy if both are comfortable and if there is a healthy amount of spontaneity and flexibility on both our parts.

This dynamic also allows us to vary our healthy roles, rituals and habits whenever it may be comfortable and appropriate.

MUTUALITY VS. PURSUING AND DISTANCING

In a healthy relationship there is an *equality* of pursuing and distancing by each partner, which is called *mutuality*. The other contacts me and initiates communications, get-togethers and activities about as often as I do. There is mutuality. [33, 67]

In a less healthy relationship, I may do most of the pursuing and the other may do most of the distancing —or the reverse. Have you ever been in such a relationship? How does it feel to be relating in this way? What might your feelings and your observations about these basic dynamics mean about your participation in the relationship? Are you getting what you want and need in the relationship? To get what we want and need in any relationship, we can be assertive and, when appropriate, set healthy boundaries and limits.

BOUNDARIES AND LIMITS VS. FUSION AND ENMESHMENT

Boundaries and limits are a central and often crucial dynamic linking these other 11 basic dynamics in relationships. If I have a good working, experiential knowledge of healthy boundaries and limits —and of my Real Self and its wants and needs— I will likely have used some boundaries and limits, consciously or unconsciously, by now in our relationship. And if I don't, I can now begin to learn about healthy boundaries and how to use them constructively in my relationships. If I don't experientially know about boundaries and if I don't use them, I may end up fused or enmeshed in a relationship. Fused or enmeshed means that my boundaries are blurred with yours. I don't know where I end or where you begin. Figure 22.1 is a cartoon illustration of a major factor in the genesis of fusion or enmeshment. We usually learn to lose our boundaries and limits in this unhealthy way from our family of origin, which this picture illustrates.

FIGURE 22.1. THE FAMILY TEACHES FUSION

I may not be clear about the difference between my feelings, wants, needs and other aspects of my inner life, and yours. I thus may not be an individuated (healthy individual) self in a healthy relationship with you. I may have lost my selfhood in you—and possibly in others—in an unhealthy way. I may feel afraid, engulfed, smothered, empty and lost.

Several other terms are similar to and may help further describe fusion or enmeshment: over-involved, clinging, walking on eggs, over-responsible, needing to control, triangle, pushes buttons, high tolerance for inappropriate behavior, frustration, fear of abandonment, feeling obligated, can't say no, all-or-none, weighted down, stuck, resentment, taken advantage of, loose boundaries, rigid boundaries, unfinished business and repetition compulsion. In each of these states there is usually some degree of fusion or enmeshment.

And what we learn, we can unlearn. As I heal, I discover my blurred and unhealthy boundaries, my fusions and enmeshments. I notice them. Progressively, more and more often, I notice how I feel when they happen and how these and other unhealthy boundaries are associated. If I choose to stop suffering unnecessarily, I can begin to set healthy boundaries and limits with others. I may now be discovering even more that my healthy boundaries and limits serve to protect and maintain the well-being and integrity of my True Self.

INTIMACY OR CLOSENESS VS. LIMITED ACQUAINTANCE & SUPERFICIALITY

Once I have a sense of myself and more about you in our relationship—and of some of each of our wants and needs—I can continue to decide and to choose just how close I want to be with you or another.

AN *INTIMATE* RELATIONSHIP

Do I want an intimate relationship with you? I define an intimate relationship as one in which two people are real with one another over time. They dare to be vulnerable and to share their True Self with each other. An intimate relationship works most successfully when both partners move toward realizing or actualizing their True Self, i.e., they are each healing and progressively in touch with their inner life. While an intimate relationship requires risking and commitment, and can frequently be scary, it can also help us know and experience ourself and our Higher Power more fully and deeply. In an intimate relationship I will have to *let go* of my boundaries more often. At other times, when appropriate, I will *set* and maintain healthy boundaries and limits.

A *CLOSE* RELATIONSHIP

In a close relationship I may let down my boundaries and share with you, but not as much or as often as I would in an intimate one. In an intimate relationship I may share more dimensions of my life, including especially my inner life, than in a close relationship.

Marilyn Mason (1988) has described nine life areas in relationships, as shown in Table 22.2 below. We can experience a closeness in any of these areas, and doing so can feel as though it is an intimate experience. But that does not make it an intimate relationship. Mason says an intimate relationship exists when we have shared in *at least four* or *five* of these nine life areas with someone with the *expectation* that the experiences and the relationship will continue over time. [34, 65]

TABLE 22.2 LIFE AREAS THAT MAY BE SHARED IN RELATIONSHIPS

Life Area	Example
1. Social	Sharing with an individual or a group
2. Intellectual	Sharing ideas or thoughts
3. Emotional	Sharing feelings
4. Physical	Working together on a physical project
5. Recreational	Sharing a recreational activity
6. Aesthetic	Sharing about what is beautiful or artistic
7. Affectional	Sharing affection via touch, tenderness or caring
8. Sexual	Requires a prior relationship
9. Spiritual	Sharing a spiritual experience

Mason says, "Most of us have learned the cultural myth that we will meet someone special who will fill all our needs. But that would keep us dependent on others to fill us up. There is no one person who can meet all our needs; a healthy individual is one who can share a variety of experiences —with more than one other person. We need friends in our lives to support us and to walk with us."

I describe close and intimate relationships in more detail throughout this book.

RELATIONSHIP AND FAMILY HEALTH VS. FAMILY DYSFUNCTION

We learn most about these basic dynamics —including boundaries, core issues and relationships— from our family of origin. We also learn many of these outside of our family, in our society of origin. Most dysfunctional families model and teach unhealthy boundaries and other dynamics. The more unhealthy, troubled or dysfunctional the family, the more likely there will be distorted and unhealthy boundaries, basic dynamics and core issues in the family members, including each of the children.

Barbara grew up in a moderately dysfunctional family, where, like most such families, the family norm was to be fused and enmeshed regarding personal boundaries. One of the main ways that her mother got attention, and at the same time tried to control and manipulate others, was to be repeatedly sick and have many medical and surgical procedures. At age 31, early in her recovery as an adult child of this dysfunctional family, Barbara—with the help of a hospital admitting clerk—set one of her first healthy boundaries with her mother. "I was irritable and depressed. I had withdrawn weeks earlier, after my third hospitalization. Besides traction, the chief of neurosurgery had performed a rhizotomy, a nerve block on my lower back, to try to stop the pain from getting worse. My doctor was highly respected, a legend at Beaumont Hospital. My mother was also seeing him, and she was admitted at the same time I was for the same procedure. We laughed about the coincidence, but it seemed weird to me. My mother asked that we share a semiprivate room in the admitting office as I sat next to her. The woman behind the desk had said `No' almost immediately. I was relieved. I knew I needed to take care of myself. No one knew what would happen, and I just didn't have the strength to take care of my mother now."

As she describes in her books *Full Circle* and *Spiritual Awakenings*, over the next 16 years Barbara Harris continued to heal as an adult child and co-dependent. And as part of her healing she learned to set healthy boundaries and limits, especially with her family of origin. This freed her to have healthy relationships with others.

HEALTHY SELF-CARING VS. UNHEALTHY NARCISSISM

Narcissism is focusing on myself and on getting my wants and needs met. It can be healthy or unhealthy. When healthy, we can call it self-caring or healthy narcissism. Without hurting another, we care for our healthy wants and needs in our own way and in our own time.

Unhealthy narcissism is focusing on self to the detriment of others (the opposite of co-dependence).[83] This detriment may be manifested and characterized by a number of behaviors and dynamics, as shown in Table 22.3 on the next page. While *some* of these unhealthy traits may be present at times in ordinary active co-dependence, and while *several* of them may be present in other personality disorders (e.g., antisocial and borderline personality disorder), and in active addictions, *most* of them tend to be present in people with narcissistic personality disorder. Because of this association, the terms "narcissism" and "narcissistic" have taken on a negative connotation, even though narcissism as *appropriate* self-*focusing* and self-*caring* can be healthy.

TABLE 22.3. CHARACTERISTICS OF HEALTHY AND UNHEALTHY NARCISSISM

Characteristic	Healthy	Unhealthy
Orientation	True Self	Negative ego
Humility	Present	Absent; ego inflated
Assertion	Self assertive	Aggressive
Boundaries	Present and Healthy	Unhealthy; often invades others'
Indulgence	Self-indulgent (as appropriate)	Selfish
Character defects	Owns character defects	Tends to project own character defects onto others
Sees others	As separate individuals with own wants, needs and feelings	Primarily as how others can be useful to them
Responsibility	Assumes appropriate personal responsibility	Blames others, avoids personal responsibility
Need to control	Values balance over control	Seeks to control or dominate
Self awareness	Self-aware of inner life	Tends to be unaware (numb) or hypersensitive
Sensitivity	Sensitive to perceived criticism or rejection	Hypersensitive to criticism or rejection
Anger	Expresses appropriately	Inappropriate anger or rage or holds it in & fumes
Honesty	Tends to be honest	Often dishonest
Empathy	Feels and expresses	Lacks
Flexibility	Realistic and flexible	Perfectionistic
Values	Values realness, relationship, positivity & creativity	Values "power," beauty, money & attention
Being around them is:	Enlivening	Toxic and draining

The person with unhealthy narcissism is acting the way our parents probably meant when they used the term "selfish" and told us "not to be that way." Yet what many of our parents didn't teach us was healthy self-caring. Before I can be in a healthy relationship, I have to know how to care for my self in a healthy way. Part of the way I can do so is by having healthy boundaries.

People with unhealthy narcissism frequently invade others' boundaries. Unless they work long and hard through an appropriate full recovery program, it is highly unlikely that they will change and become healthily self-caring.

And so it may be difficult, if not impossible, ever to have a healthy and fulfilling relationship with them. As an example, the

following shows an interaction between the two basic dynamics of boundaries and narcissism.

Audrey, a caretaker and people-pleaser, was married to Max, a self-centered rageaholic. Both were unrecovered adult children of unhealthy families. After three years of tolerating his repeated inappropriate behavior, which involved excluding her from decisions about their home and outbursts of rage at her when she tried to express her wants and needs around all this, Audrey began therapy for her resulting frustration and pain. After six months of weekly individual psychotherapy, she joined a trauma focused therapy group.

A year later she realized that her frustration was not only with Max. She was also enmeshed with her narcissistic, rageaholic father and with a narcissistic and a shaming boss. Over the next year she began to care for herself further (healthy narcissism) by setting limits on all three. She told both her father and Max that she would no longer speak to them when they raged at her, and she became more assertive with her boss. While her puzzled and upset father kept his distance, Max had an affair and then reluctantly entered counseling with her. After eight sessions, half of which Max did not attend, she decided to separate from him —another healthy boundary.

Further work in group helped her discover that not only had she *not* been taught about healthy boundaries in her family of origin, but she had grown up in a mentally and emotionally enmeshed family. To survive, she had used her false self that manifested in a caretaker role, which she had carried into her marriage and work.

After four years of recovery, she now has a strong sense of her True Self. Part of her continued self-caring (healthy narcissism) is using boundaries and limits to protect it. Still attending group therapy, she got herself transferred to another boss and is awaiting the finalization of her divorce in five months.

CONTENT VS. PROCESS

Content and process have to do with the communication, experience and reaction within any relationship. Content includes what specific words and sentences are said. Process is all other forms of communication that occur in the relationship, including our reactions, responses, behaviors and all other *non-verbal* ways of communicating. As with most of the basic dynamics, both of these may be used in either a healthy or an unhealthy way.

Each of these basic dynamics and the core recovery issues can interact with each other in various ways. For example, boundaries may interact with content and process at the level of the core issue of high tolerance for inappropriate behavior. This can be illustrated in the relationship of a married couple, Clay and Sally, both adult children of trauma and chemical dependent.

Clay was in a full recovery program for his chemical dependence, and Sally was not. In fact, although she was ordered by the court to be abstinent from alcohol and drugs and to be in a recovery program, she was still drinking. She was so dysfunctional that she frequently called Clay from a bar or a friend's home at three in the morning to come pick her up and to pay for her drinking or drug-using bill, even though she knew he had to work the next day to support them. His boundaries were so loose that he tolerated this inappropriate behavior for over a year, picking her up and paying her bills. In spite of his occasionally *telling* her of his frustration and hurt (*content*), his *behavior* (*process*) of not setting healthy boundaries and limits cancelled all of his best-intentioned words.

Clay required many sessions working in group therapy during this time to see what was happening and how his own behavior was not only enabling Sally to continue being actively addicted, but was also endangering his own recovery and disrupting his life. He finally realized that his most healthy choice was to care for himself, and he separated from her. She moved in with her sister and continued to go downhill in her active addiction. While he was strongly tempted several times to get back together with her, with the help of his therapy group and AA sponsor, he was able to maintain these healthy boundaries and to grow in his own recovery as both a recovering chemical dependent and co-dependent.

I chose this story of Clay and Sally, an extreme example of disordered content and process, to illustrate them more clearly. Content and process in most relationships are less dramatic and more subtle. Because of this subtlety, it can be helpful to monitor what is going on inside you and in the relationship and to ask your partner if they would be willing to do the same. Indeed, because process can be so powerful and because much of it may go on inside our own heads, whether as fantasy or not, in any relationship it can be helpful to check in frequently about what may be real and what is not for each other. To do so may require risking being vulnerable, or opening a boundary, to bring up the particular subject or concern.

GROWTH VS. STAGNATION OR REGRESSION

When we heal, we grow. When we live from and as our True Self, we are free to explore, connect, reflect, learn, struggle, experience, create, celebrate, enjoy and just *be*. Healthy boundaries protect our True Self so it can stay out and be and do and experience all of these, thereby evolving and growing.

When our True Self goes into hiding and stays there, we cannot grow. Without healthy boundaries, our Child Within may be too scared or hurt to come out. And so we stagnate or regress. Instead of being and feeling like a Hero or Heroine, as described above, we may feel like a martyr or a victim, trapped and unhappy. Discovering and using these basic dynamics and core issues boundaries can help us to come out of hiding and be real, as our True Self, and to grow and experience peace.

CONCLUSION

In this chapter I have briefly described some important basic dynamics in relationships. Being aware of, understanding and using these may help us make our relationships and lives more successful and fun. Having a clear awareness of our inner and outer life and healthy boundaries and limits in the relationship, as in each of these basic dynamics, will help maintain a healthy balance of the two sides or dimensions of each specific basic dynamic.

APPENDIX

TABLE A.1. "EGO" DEFENSES — A SUMMARY*

Defense	Description	Example
Denial	arguing against an anxiety/fear-provoking stimulus by saying it doesn't exist	denying that a diagnosis of cancer is correct even after a second opinion
Projection	placing unacceptable impulses from within yourself onto someone else	when clearly losing a fact based argument, you say "You're just stupid"
Displace-ment	taking out impulses on a less threatening target	slamming a door instead of hitting a person, yelling at your spouse after an argument with your boss
Intellect-ualization	avoiding unacceptable emotions by focusing on the intellectual aspects	focusing on the details of a funeral as opposed to the sadness and grief

---

Defense	Description	Example
Rational-ization	supplying a logical or rational reason as opposed to the real reason	saying that you were fired because you didn't kiss up the boss, when the real reason was your poor performance
Reaction formation	taking the opposite belief because the true belief causes fear and anxiety	altruism hides selfishness; piety conceals sinfulness; co-operation hides rage
Regress-ion	returning to a previous stage of development	throwing a temper tantrum when you don't get your way
Repress-ion	Unconscious storage into the unconscious	forgetting a severe trauma due to the fear and anxiety
Suppress-ion	Conscious pushing into the unconscious	trying to forget something that causes you anxiety
Sublima-tion	acting out unacceptable impulses in a socially acceptable way	sublimating your aggressive impulses toward a career as a boxer

*Modified from
allpsych.com/psychology101/defenses.html

If you have *not answered* the next Core Issues Recovery Potential Survey, it may be helpful to look at it now or soon.

TABLE A.2. CORE ISSUES
RECOVERY POTENTIAL SURVEY

Circle or check the word **that most applies to** how you *truly* believe, experience or feel.

1. Do you seek approval and affirmation?
> Never   Seldom   Occasionally   Often   Usually

2. If you can't do something perfectly, how often do you just *not* do it.
> Never   Seldom   Occasionally   Often   Usually

3. Do you fear criticism?
> Never   Seldom   Occasionally   Often   Usually

4. Do you overextend yourself?
> Never   Seldom   Occasionally   Often   Usually

5. Have you had problems with your own compulsive behavior?
> Never   Seldom   Occasionally   Often   Usually

6. **Do you have a need for perfection?**
> Never   Seldom   Occasionally   Often   Usually

7. **Do you attend more to others than to your own wants and needs?**
> Never   Seldom   Occasionally   Often   Usually

8. **Do you have difficulty expressing painful feelings after a big hurt, loss or trauma?**
> Never   Seldom   Occasionally   Often   Usually

9. **Do you care for others easily, yet find it difficult to care for yourself?**
> Never   Seldom   Occasionally   Often   Usually

11. **Do you respond with anxiety to authority figures and angry people?**
> Never   Seldom   Occasionally   Often   Usually

12. **Do you feel that individuals and society in general are taking advantage of you?**
    Never   Seldom   Occasionally   Often   Usually

13. **Do you have trouble with intimate relationships?**
    Never   Seldom   Occasionally   Often   Usually

14. **Do you attract people who tend to abuse you?**
    Never   Seldom   Occasionally   Often   Usually

15. **Do you cling to relationships because you are afraid of being alone?**
    Never   Seldom   Occasionally   Often   Usually

16. **Do you mistrust your own feelings and feelings expressed by others?**
    Never   Seldom   Occasionally   Often   Usually

17. **Do you find it difficult to express your emotions?**
    Never   Seldom   Occasionally   Often   Usually

18. **Do you give to others more than they give to you?**
    Never   Seldom   Occasionally   Often   Usually

19. **Do you find yourself compulsively eating, drinking, working, using drugs or seeking excitement?**
    Never   Seldom   Occasionally   Often   Usually

20. **Do you fear any of the following:**
a. **Losing control?**
    Never   Seldom   Occasionally   Often   Usually
b. **Your own feelings?**
    Never   Seldom   Occasionally   Often   Usually
c. **Conflict and criticism?**
    Never   Seldom   Occasionally   Often   Usually

d. **Being rejected or abandoned**?
    Never   Seldom   Occasionally   Often   Usually

e. **Being a failure**?
    Never   Seldom   Occasionally   Often   Usually

21. **Have you tried counseling or psychotherapy yet "something" is wrong or missing?**
    Never   Seldom   Occasionally   Often   Usually

22. **Do you frequently feel numb, empty or sad?**
    Never   Seldom   Occasionally   Often   Usually

23. **Is it hard for you to trust others?**
    Never   Seldom   Occasionally   Often   Usually

24. **Do you have an over-developed sense of responsibility?**
    Never   Seldom   Occasionally   Often   Usually

25. **Do you feel a lack of fulfillment in life, personally and in your work?**
    Never   Seldom   Occasionally   Often   Usually

26. **Do you have feelings of guilt, inadequacy or low self esteem?**
    Never   Seldom   Occasionally   Often   Usually

27. **Do you have a tendency toward having chronic fatigue, aches and pains?**
    Never   Seldom   Occasionally   Often   Usually

28. **Do you find that it is difficult to visit your parents for more than a few minutes or a few hours?**
    Never   Seldom   Occasionally   Often   Usually

29. **Are you hesitant to respond when people ask about your feelings?**
    Never   Seldom   Occasionally   Often   Usually

30. **Have you wondered if you were mistreated or neglected as a child?**
    Never   Seldom   Occasionally   Often   Usually

31. **Do you have difficulty asking for what you want or need from others?**
    Never   Seldom   Occasionally   Often   Usually

32. **Do you feel guilty around others?**
    Never   Seldom   Occasionally   Often   Usually

33. **Have you had difficulty expressing or giving and receiving love?**
    Never   Seldom   Occasionally   Often   Usually

If you answered "Occasionally" "Often" or "Usually" to any of these questions, this book may be helpful to you. If you answered mostly "Never," you may not be aware of some of your issues.

TABLE A.3. CHECKLIST FOR IDENTIFYING SOME OF MY CORE ISSUES BASED ON ABOVE SURVEY

Core Issue	Survey Items *	Comments
Control	6, 20a,	Major early in recovery
Trust	13, 23,	Learn to trust safe people only
Being real	13, 31	Key to & necessary for healing
Feelings	5, 11, 16, 17, 19, 22, 29, 32	Double-edged sword
Low self-esteem (*aka* shame)	6, 13, 14, 20e, 26	Result of all abuse & neglect
Dependence	15	Healthy v. unhealthy
Fear of abandonment	10, 15, 20d,	Major issue. Key link to all other CIs

Core Issue	Survey Items *	Comments
High tolerance for inappropriate behavior	4, 14, 18,	Common in all levels of relationships
Over-responsibility for others	9, 18, 24, 32	Key issue in co-dependence
Neglecting my own needs	18, 25, 31	Common basic trauma effect
Grieving my ungrieved losses	20b, 22,	Helps our recovery go best over time
Difficulty resolving conflict	3, 7, 9, 11, 14, 15, 17, 18, 20 b-e, 23, 31, 32	Common, Key issue to know and address
Difficulty giving & receiving love	3, 11, 14, 20c	Common in intimate relationships Perhaps *the* key issue *later* in recovery
Other items	13, 33	Common in intimate relationships
	19, 21,27, 28,30	These suggest you probably have more Core Issues *

* When you answered occasionally, often or usually for any item.

An answer of "Never" to any item may indicate that you are in denial of the question or issue.

These questions and checklist are useful only to *get you started* in exploring your core issues, and if you choose sharing it with selected safe people such as your therapist, or sponsor.

TABLE A.4. STAGES of RECOVERY, FOCUS AND DURATION [99,103]

Stage	Condition	Focus	Approximate Duration
3	Human/spiritual	Spirituality	Ongoing
2	Past trauma effects	Trauma-specific recovery program	3–5+ years
1	Stage 0 disorder	Basic illness, full recovery program	Months to 3 years
0	Active illness	Usually none	Indefinite

*Note that this table reads from bottom to top

THE STAGES OF RECOVERY

While all acute injuries need some time to heal, *chronic* ones such as PTSD and the like tend to *take more time*.

STAGE ZERO

Stage Zero is active illness, and here recovery has not yet begun. It is manifested by the presence of any active disorder, such as a mental or physical one, including "depression," an addiction or any other problem. In this stage, you see both symptoms and signs and other *effects of whatever caused* the illness. This active illness may be acute, recurring or chronic. Without recovery, it may continue indefinitely—unless the person becomes somehow motivated to begin a Stage One effort. At Stage Zero, recovery has not yet started, as shown in Table A.4 above.

STAGE ONE

Coming to treatment for any mental or physical disorder is the beginning of Stage One. It involves participating in a partial (usual) or full (ideal) recovery program to assist in healing the Stage Zero disorder. It is the standard kind of process that we most commonly consider as conventional psychiatric or medical "treatment." If you are diabetic, you treat the diabetes by handling your diet, exercising, taking insulin and so forth.

If you had "depression," you would often simply be prescribed an antidepressant drug, with little or no investigation as to its cause. Depending on the person and the problem, such a partial recovery program may be less likely to be as successful as a more complete regimen, which includes a Stage Two program. Stage One is the usual conventional, superficial treatment of mental disorders by using drugs alone. But that limited approach often does not work well. That is because most Stage One people usually come in with a presenting problem or concern that is actually the effect of the repeated trauma, addressed next. [99,103]

STAGE TWO

The typical motivation for beginning Stage One recovery is hurting too much—emotional pain, physical pain or debilitating disease. But eventually, somewhere during, or more often after, Stage One recovery, people may realize that they are still hurting. They realize that whatever they have done before hasn't worked as well as they had hoped—that the Stage One approach alone (drugs, surgery, etc) didn't help them enough. So they might then be more open to exploring other alternatives. That is where they can begin a more substantial healing—*if* they are able to find a helping professional who *knows* Stage Two work.

Stage Two recovery involves naming, working through, and healing the effects of repeated childhood and later trauma, including working through related core issues. Once a person has a stable and solid Stage One recovery—one that has lasted for at least a few months to a year or longer—it may be time to consider looking into some of these Stage Two issues. Some mental disorders, especially those such as addictions (which commonly aggravate depression and anxiety), some personality disorders, dissociative disorders and psychoses usually require a year or more to *reach* enough *stability* to be able to engage in Stage Two work. A trauma survivor may have grown up in an unhealthy, troubled or dysfunctional family. Many survivors may still be in a similar unhealthy environment, whether at home, in one or more relationships, or at work.

How long does the Stage Two recovery process typically take? For a history of trauma that has become entrenched, which most are, it can take years to heal enough to find lasting peace. For some it may take less time. There is no requirement or judgment on the amount of time it takes for a person to recover. It takes as long as it takes. My 30-plus years of experience in leading trauma-specific therapy groups has been that the members continually find relief when *working* and even when simply *listening* to others' work. In *A Gift to Myself*, I include numerous guidelines and experiential exercises to help facilitate Stage Two work, with a section at the end on how to access when it may be time to stop therapy.

It is helpful to make a personal recovery plan, a point I have emphasized throughout my prior books. Making such a recovery plan gives us lots of advantages as we heal, one of which is to discover the usefulness of naming things accurately (see the Chapter, "Naming Things Accurately," in *A Gift to Myself* for details). [92]

For example, instead of "depression," if appropriate, consider calling it *grieving* from major losses and/or childhood trauma. And instead of saying "I deserved it," consider calling it abuse or trauma. These kinds of reframes can be effective as we heal. Doing so is important because what we deal with in therapy is often actually grieving, or stuck grief, and not "depression" or another "mental disorder." "Depression" and "mental disorder" involve *Stage Zero* and *Stage One thinking*, and reframing depression as stuck grief—that is, needing to grieve but being somehow blocked from doing it—would be more accurate Stage Two thinking and understanding. As a therapist or patient/client, coming from that understanding, we can see the need to help people identify and accurately name exactly what they are grieving from or about, thereby aiding them in their healing in a healthy way.

What about a person who can't do more therapy because of managed care restrictions, budget constraints, low income and so on? We do the best with what we have. People who are motivated to heal can be creative. That's one reason *I wrote my books*—that is, *for my patients*, so they could save time and money by learning how to do the healing themselves, although with the help of safe others, including some safe therapists, and those not pushing psychiatric drugs. Often, people go from one therapist to another, like people do with attempted intimate relationships. Some fit. Others don't. They learn as much as they can with one teacher or guide and then go on to the next. [99,103]

STAGE THREE

Stage Three recovery involves spirituality and its incorporation into our daily life. Folding this strong recovery aid into our everyday flow is an ongoing and lifelong process. Stage Three is learning to realize spirituality. It is expanding the same question, "Who am I?" from Stage Two work, since that is a central question there, too. In Stage Three, the person is continuing to work on "Who am I?" in a deeper way. But now we also expand that question, "Who am I?" to the next interesting one: "What am I doing here?" and then "Where am I going?" Actually, Stage Three encompasses the whole process, from Stage Zero onward. Everything we do is spiritual, and by spiritual I am not talking about religion. I'm talking about relationships and experiences with self, others, and the Divine Mystery or God/Goddess/All-That-Is. Spirituality is about making meaning that may involve different levels of our life.

Spirituality is a powerful tool. Many people confuse spirituality with religion. While religions are kinds of "brand names," spirituality is the generic umbrella that embraces and transcends all religions. [103,104]

Table A .5. Schemas / Lifetraps and Core Issues Expand and Support One Another[80]

Core Issue	Schema/Lifetrap Related to Core Issues
Control	**1a. Unrelenting Standards** The core message of the unrelenting standards lifetrap is, "I must work very hard to meet very high standards or I will be criticized. I do not have time to relax or have too much fun. I must always be efficient." The driving words for this lifetrap are "I should …"
	1b. Insufficient Self-Control The core message of the insufficient self-control lifetrap is, "I should not be uncomfortable." This lifetrap leads people to express their emotion negatively, avoid difficult tasks, and give in to temptation. This lifetrap interferes with healthy adult behavior of reciprocity in relationships, and setting and achieving goals.
	1c. Vulnerability The core message of the vulnerability lifetrap is, "Catastrophe is just around the corner. Bad things are about to happen and I am powerless to do anything about it."
Trust	**2. Mistrust/Abuse** The core message of the mistrust lifetrap is, "I cannot expect others to treat me in a fair, considerate or just manner. I should expect to be hurt (emotionally or even physically), lied to, taken advantage

	of, and manipulated. Others have their own agenda."
Being real	**3a. Emotional Inhibition** The core message of the emotional inhibition lifetrap is, "I should not express myself or show my emotions. I should always be in control."
	3b. Approval-Seeking The core message of the approval-seeking lifetrap is, "I must seek the approval of others above all else. If other people do not approve of me, something is very wrong." This pattern of thinking is about defining who we are through the eyes of others rather than paying attention to our own needs and desires.
Feelings	**4. Emotional Deprivation** The core message of the emotional deprivation lifetrap is, "I cannot expect others to be supportive of me and care about what I need." Emotional deprivation is about insufficient empathy, nurturing, and/or not receiving guidance and direction.
Low self-esteem	**5a. Defectiveness** The core message of the defectiveness lifetrap is, "I am not good enough. I am inherently flawed. Anyone who truly knows me could not love me."
	5b. Failure The core message of the failure lifetrap is, "I am fundamentally incompetent and have failed, am failing, and will fail again

Low self-esteem ... continued	in the future. I am less talented and successful than other people." The focus of this lifetrap is on achievement and external status symbols of success, rather than on the internal feeling of shame and inferiority that is present in the case of the defectiveness lifetrap.
	5c. Social Isolation The core message of the social isolation lifetrap is, "I am different from other people and do not fit in." The feelings of isolation and being alone stem from feeling apart from any group or community, and too different to belong.
	5d. Unrelenting Standards_ – *See under* 1. Control *above*
Dependence	**6a. Dependence** The core message of the dependence lifetrap is, "I cannot take care of myself. I need to rely on those around me in order to survive. I cannot solve problems or make decisions on my own."
	6b. Enmeshment The core message of the enmeshment lifetrap is, "I cannot survive on my own without constant contact and closeness with my parent or partner. I need to know what they think in order to be sure of what I think." This is about an underdeveloped sense of self as a separate person.

Fear of abandonment	**7. Abandonment** The core message of the abandonment lifetrap is, "I cannot count on anyone for consistent support, caring, and connection. I will be rejected; people I love and need will die; and people I love and need cannot be relied upon to be there when I need them."
All-or-none thinking and behaving	**8a. Unrelenting Standards** – *See under* 1. Control *above*
	8b. Negativity/Pessimism The core message of the negativity lifetrap is, "I am destined to make a serious mistake that will result in big problems. Things will inevitably go wrong. Bad things will happen to me." The negative aspects of life are emphasized at the expense of those things which are positive and potentially joy-bringing.
	8c. Punitiveness The core message of the punitiveness lifetrap is, "Mistakes have consequences —I should be punished for making mistakes and so should everyone else. It is not okay to make a mistake. We should constantly strive for and demand perfection."
High tolerance for inappropriate behavior	**9a. Mistrust/Abuse** – *See under* 2. Trust *above*
	9b. Subjugation The core message of the subjugation lifetrap is, "I must submit to the needs and desires of others before my own or I will be rejected by

	the anger or abandonment of people who are important to me." The internal slogan is "I'm number two." Subjugation is about needs— not showing preferences, desires, decisions and opinions, or emotions—not showing feelings, particularly anger.
Over-responsibility for others	10a. **Self-Sacrifice** The core message of the self-sacrifice lifetrap is, "I must meet the needs of others before my own. I do not want to feel selfish or cause any pain to others." This pattern of thinking and behaving appears very kind but creates problems in the long run as it results in imbalanced relationships, and problems with unmet needs.
	10b. **Enmeshment** – *See under* 6. Dependence *above*
Neglecting my own needs	11a. **Self-Sacrifice** – *See under* 10. Over-responsibility *above*
	11b. **Subjugation** – *See under* 9. High tolerance *above*
Grieving my ungrieved losses	12a. **Emotional Inhibition** – *See under* 3. Being Real *above*
	12b. **Unrelenting Standards** – *See under* 1. Control *above*
Difficulty resolving conflict	13a. **Subjugation** – *See under* 9. High tolerance *above*
	13b. **Entitlement** The core message of the entitlement

	lifetrap is, "I am special and better than other people. Rules should not apply to me. I should always come first. "This lifetrap is rooted in a desire for power and control.
Difficulty giving and receiving love	14a. **Emotional Deprivation** – *See under* 4. Feelings *above*
	15b. **Defectiveness** – *See under* 5. Low Self-esteem *above*
	14c. **Self-Sacrifice** – *See under* 10. Over-responsibility *above*

From Louis J, Schema therapist, based on www.schematherapy.com/id201.htm [80]

SECTION A.1. TOXIC TEASING

This describes another example in the spectrum of how people shame one another, especially in families and some groups. Some possible punchline terms: "If you can't take a joke" or simplified as "Gotcha"—or you might fill-in-the-blank

_____

This kind of shaming is done most commonly in a group of 3 or more people, which suggests that when two of the group are alone together they may get along better because there is no audience to support the toxic behavior.

Similar to classical triangles, participants usually consist of: **abuser**, **victim** and **observer(s).** The abuser usually first has to identify some characteristic of the victim to call attention to a victim flaw, a painful memory, or a past or current mistake. The abuser may also use sarcasm.

The purpose of the game is to break the tension within the abuser and/or the observing group at the time just before the toxic teasing. This dynamic can take several guises. An example would be: instead of honestly expressing hurt, fear or anger, 1 on 1 in private with an individual, the abuser waits until *others are present* and then attacks and embarrasses or humiliates the victim. Then the abuser can deny any responsibility by saying, "I was just kidding," or "Can't you take a joke?"

Often the abuser is insecure, coming from their *own* unhealed shame. This game is subtle, hidden or covert so that many times the others don't know about the abuser's insecurity because they hide it so well. This hiding is made possible by the abuser distracting and projecting their insecurities on others.

This dynamic is so simple, devious and pervasive that it is not always easy to identify when it is happening until later, if ever. The emotional abuse leaves the victim feeling shamed, embarrassed, attacked and confused —and sometimes overwhelmed—because there's usually no way at the time for them to be aware of and identify what has actually happened. If they try, they are made to look foolish and all the above feelings often repeat, and they are left with a sense of having no way out.

The victim is often already in the middle of an age regression which immobilizes them and they are unable to respond appropriately. Others in the family or group who are observing this emotional abuse-in-action are trained and sometimes even brainwashed to *laugh* at the key "gotcha" word, phrase or "if you can't take a joke." When the victim tries to protest, the abuser and the whole observing group will come back with more shaming, claiming that the victim doesn't have a sense of humor.

The set up goes something like this: The emotional abuser introduces an opinion or makes up something that is shaming about the victim in the guise of being funny, light-hearted or humorous—when in fact, underneath they are trying to break *their own* internal tension. The "funny" remark will often try to call attention to a fault, trait, characteristic or painful memory about the victim.

Already feeling hurt and often age-regressed, the victim may try to neutralize the statement, only to dig themselves into a hole because they've let themselves become engaged in the toxic teasing process.

They become entrenched in the "joke."

The victim either dissociates, runs away or tries to identify what is going on, including or possibly identifying the abuser as an abuser. But that doesn't usually work.

Others who are present or watching may join in because, like the abuser, they become energized and continue with yet more abuse that they consider "funny" to release more tension. Of course, this is using humor in an unhealthy and mean way.

Viewing this scenario from the perspective of triangles, the usual triangle dynamic is that the *rescuer* comes to support the *victim* (bottom of page 289 below). But in this toxic teasing the otherwise classical triangle's rescuer but now third party/observing group intervenes in *supporting* the *abuser* by laughing at their "joke." This is a reversal of the usual perpetrator-victim-rescuer dynamic. The way out of triangles is to have healthy one-on-one relationships. Toxic teasing distracts from the tension and conflict between the abuser and the victim if the abuser were to be real with the victim one-on-one.

The abuser is also usually a bully. Toxic teasing is another guise of bullying behavior, which uses force or coercion to try to overpower others. Bullying consists of three basic types of abuse: emotional, verbal, and physical. They may use verbal harassment, physical assault or coercion and may target certain victims, based on a person's physical size, appearance, religion, race, gender, sexuality, other preferences or their inability to set limits. Bullying ranges from simple one-on-one bullying to more complex bullying in which the bully may have one or more 'lieutenants' who may seem to be willing to assist the primary bully in their bullying activities. The victim of bullying is sometimes referred to as a "target."

Example of the toxic teasing:

- Abuser: Yea! Your last boyfriend, was married.
  And your boyfriend before him —Married too.
- Victim: Stop that. I didn't know they were married until later.
- Abuser: No. You're just a married man magnet!
- Others Laugh.
- Victim: That's not funny!
- Abuser: Well, if you can't take a joke...
- Others: Oh! Common! He's only teasing!

Fill in the blank with any examples you have

seen an abuser employ. As an experiential exercise, consider the following:

Write about your experiences of witnessing bullying associated with triangles, only this time the third party doesn't try to rescue the victim, but rescues the abuser by laughing.

Describe how the tension is released on to the victim. Include any examples you have seen an abuser employ. Take your time.

SECTION A.2. DIFFICULTY HANDLING CONFLICT
FIVE GENERAL FACTORS

Relationship conflicts usually occur because of our strong painful feelings and emotions, misperceptions, misunderstandings, mis-communications, or repetitive upsetting behaviors. These factors often fuel disputes and an unnecessary increasing spiral of painful and destructive conflict. But with an increased awareness we can use that pain to motivate us to work through and solve the conflict.

Information or **Data** conflicts occur when we • lack enough information necessary to make wise decisions, • are misinformed, • disagree on which data are relevant, • interpret it differently, or • have competing views. Some of these may be unnecessary since they are caused or aggravated by poor communication between us and others. Every conflict has two sides. Of course, we may collect, interpret or communicate information differently.

Interest conflicts are caused by competition over perceived incompatible wants or needs. Conflicts-of-interest result when one or more of us believe that in order to satisfy our interests, that the wants, needs and interests of an *opponent* are not important. Our interests may involve • *substantive* issues (such as money, physical resources, time, attention, etc.); • *procedural* issues (the way we can resolve the conflict); and • *psychological* issues (other core issues as trust, control, all-or-none, and other factors as fairness, choice to participate, respect and unconscious dynamics such as projection).

Structural conflicts involve factors and forces outside of those in dispute. Limited physical resources, geographic constraints, time (too little or too much), organization changes, and the like can make it seem like a crisis, when it may not be. Our conflicts will often have structural *solutions*. Parties' appreciation that a conflict has an external source can allow us to jointly address and solve it.

In **Value** conflicts we see incompatible belief systems. Values are beliefs that we use to give meaning to our lives. They put in plain words what we see as "good" or "bad," "right" or "wrong," "just" or "unjust" (and thus can have an all-or-none sense). Differing values need not cause conflict. We can live together fine with different value systems. Value disputes arise only when people attempt to force (control) their values onto others. It is hard to change anyone's values and belief systems.

WORKPLACE CONFLICTS

Interdependence conflicts. Our job depends on others' co-operation, output or input. For example, when a sales-person is constantly late inputting the monthly sales figures that causes the accountant to be late with their reports.

Style differences. Our styles for doing a job can differ. For example, one person may want to get the work done quickly (task oriented), while another is more concerned about having it done a particular way e.g., artistically or by including other people in the project.

Background/Gender differences. Conflicts can arise because of differences in educational backgrounds, personal experiences, ethnic heritage, gender and political preferences.

Leadership differences. Leaders often have different styles. Employees who change from one supervisor to another can get confused, for example, while one leader may be more open and inclusive, another may be more directive.

Personality clashes. These common workplace conflicts are often fueled by [mis]perceptions about others' motives and character, unaddressed core issues and by resulting emotions. For example, a team leader jumps on someone for being late because she [mis]perceives the team member as being lazy and inconsiderate. The team member sees the team leader as out to get him. Personality conflicts may cause up to 85% of worker dismissals.

SECTION A.3 POWER OF HUMILITY MAP

Level 1 Conflict is our usual conflicted state when we get caught in a conventional triangle. Occasional triangles are common, but we can learn to avoid even them. The 3 classic triangle roles include the **victim** (with which most members tend to identify), **perpetrator** (least common identification), and **rescuer** (sometimes identification). Inside the triangle members commonly experience any one or more of the spectrum of painful feelings, from fear (our society's common code word for fear is usually "anxiety") to anger, frustration (anger + fear/anxiety), guilt, shame, hurt and confusion—or more often a combination.

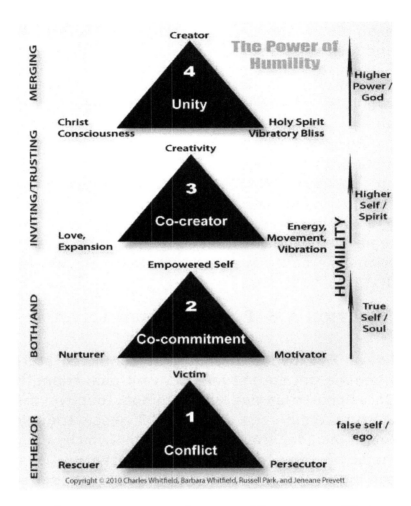

MERGING

INVITING/TRUSTING

BOTH/AND

EITHER/OR

Creator

The Power of Humility

4

Unity

Christ
Consciousness

Holy Spirit
Vibratory Bliss

Higher
Power /
God

Creativity

3

Co-creator

Love,
Expansion

Energy,
Movement,
Vibration

Higher
Self /
Spirit

Empowered Self

2

Co-commitment

Nurturer

Motivator

HUMILITY

True
Self /
Soul

Victim

1

Conflict

Rescuer

Persecutor

false self /
ego

Copyright © 2010 Charles Whitfield, Barbara Whitfield, Russell Park, and Jeneane Prevett

Level 2 = co-commitment The most efficient way to get out of this triangle-induced emotional (and sometimes physical) pain is to stop participating in the triangle. Of course the other 2 members will likely try to brand you as "the bad guy" for not staying with them in their conflicts. But don't let their labels bother you. You don't have to remain a part of this pain. For *committed* couples, *business partners* or *the like* who may get embroiled in a triangle, the two main members may consider moving to the next higher level, called **Level 2**, which is **co-commitment,** where we realize we have more choices than all-or-none. Now and here we don't have to accept painful and often disabling conflict in these kinds of relationships anymore.

Engaging the power of our inherent humility we can rise from our prior *all-or-none*, *either/or* stance in Level 1 **Conflict** to a more open, accepting and freeing experience of *both-and* and into a higher functioning level of **co-commitment**. We each commit to the likelihood and reality that there will be a better way to handle our conflict. Sometimes we may need to agree to disagree. Nonetheless, here we each (co-)commit to reframing and seeing our roles now being a 1) *motivator* instead of a perpetrator, 2) *self-empowered* instead of a victim, and a 3) *nurturer* instead of a rescuer, as we show in the Map. By thus using the power of humility, we transcend *either/or* thinking and move up to *both/and* thinking and behaving which allows us many more choices.

It can take a long time to get used to functioning at this advantageous and more peaceful level. Part of avoiding the painful conflict of being in a triangle is to focus on having healthy 2-way relationships and not triangle-in a third party.

Level 3 = Co-creator Here we transform our *empowered self* of Level 2 into a **co-creative (with God) self** with *energy* and *action*. Each of the prior roles rises still another notch (see Map). At this level of development, it's as though we become partners with God. We sense the flow and perfection of God in our life, and act to creatively manifest our now expanded intent, and we love unconditionally.

Level 4 = Unity Consciousness - Here we expand our awareness of what we call our Sacred Person: True Self, Higher Self and Higher Power or God. When we are totally alive and no longer need to spend any energy living from our ego or false self, living as our Sacred Person is Level 4 living. When we ask for help at this level, it comes almost immediately in ways we couldn't have predicted. This help comes with integrity and tenderness. We are flooded with knowledge about ourselves, the other person or the relationship. It appears like a Life Review. We feel what the other person is feeling. We see the bigger picture. And we trust God's Divine Energy to work in others as it is working in us.

from Whitfield CL, Whitfield BH, Prevatt J, Park R (2006) *The Power of Humility*: Choosing Peace over Conflict in Relationships. Health Communications, Deerfield Beach, FL

SECTION A.4 FAIR FIGHTING FOR COMMITTED COUPLES

For committed couples or partners who tend to fight unfairly they can use a structured but effective method of resolving conflicts called fair fighting (FF). This takes a lot of attention and time, but once a couple learns to do it, it becomes easier and usually more effective than unfair fighting. Here is a summary of how to do it. For more details do an online search and also see Richard Dayringer's classic article.

Fair fighting is negotiating with your spouse or partner for change in order to get what you want that will (hopefully) make your relationship more peaceful. **Unfair fighting** includes: yelling, screaming, shaming, "mind reading" (projection of one's inner life on to another), [1] threatening, using any physical aggression, "taking the other's inventory," bringing up old or off-topic complaints or parts of your "anger museum," dominating the conversation or using the "silent treatment").

Before starting or early on in the FF process it is helpful for each to write out their own "anger museum," which consists of everything they have been angry at the other about and for which they may still hold a resentment and may use for unfair fighting. Without showing it to the other, they bring their list to the next couples therapy session, read it to the other and discuss it with the therapist's input. Then the therapist asks each if they may be willing to let go of their listed resentments. If they agree, any items on this list are now unfair to use in any future arguments.

Fair fighting uses a series of steps of mutual sharing that when followed will facilitate an improved relationship. These rules and guidelines include: 1) One request or complaint at a time. 2) No unfair tactics allowed. 3) Starting with the request, each partner takes three minutes to say their request or response, while the listener remains silent. This time has to be kept mutual so that each gets the same three minutes or up to a maximum of five minutes if both agree. 4) Each exchange starts with the speaker saying what they just heard from the other, to which the prior speaker affirms or not and says "Thank you." 5) Each alternately speaks until both are complete about their expressions. 6) The invited spouse may accept the invitation, decline, or postpone it. 7) Each uses "I messages" and speaks from and as their real self. When appropriate they can use such wording as "When you say/do _____, I feel _____, because _____."

Ideally a therapist or counselor supervises or "referees" their first fight and "Huddles" with each to help with their response when need. Finally the requester asks "will you grant my request for change?" And the responder agrees or not. Or they can continue negotiating as above or agree to continue the exchange later or agree to disagree for now. The couple may finally elect to agree that a complainer cannot complain about an event longer than a week after it occurs, which tends to keep them current.

Steps to negotiate a "couple's issue" (defined by Dayringer as *displeasure from interfering with reaching a goal* as an *individual* or a *couple*) [27]

1. Engagement to Fight: invitation to accept, postpone or decline a conflict.

2. Selection of Complaint for "beef."

3. Huddle for rehearsal: strategy conference with therapist or safe/neutral 3rd party.

4. Statement of complaint to spouse/partner.

5. Feedback and reward: Restatement to clarify, other listens, mutual thanks.

6. Huddle to determine request for change: Clarification of behavior needed.

7. Request for change: request made based on clarifications.

8. Feedback and reward: other gives feedback and reward to manner of request.

9. Evocation: 1st party makes direct request, "Will you change?"

10. Huddle to consider change: 3rd party helps 2nd party decide, suggesting alternatives

11. Unconditional or conditional acceptance: acceptance or negotiation with 3rd party.

12. Planning next engagement: another engagement planned.

13.Closure: agreement becomes a commitment sealed verbally and physically (hug)/good will.

SECTION A.5 NOTES ON NEGLECTING MY OWN NEEDS

In ideal circumstances, our human needs must be fulfilled so that we can develop and grow. Drawing on authors such as Maslow (1962), Weil (1973), Miller (1983, 1984), Glasser (1985), and Reiss (2009). I compiled a list of twenty factors or conditions that I call "human needs" (Table A.6). Nearly all are associated with our relationship with ourself and with the others around us. Human needs are a central organizing construct for personality and behavior. To reach our full potential we require most of them. Growing up in an environment without them we usually don't realize that our needs have not been met and many may still not be met today. That experience often leaves us confused and unhappy.

Table A.6. A Hierarchy of Human Needs

1. Survival,
    Food,
    Physical activity
	11. Opportunity to grieve losses and to grow

2. Safety	12. Support for most of these
3. Touching, safe skin contact	13. Loyalty and trust
4. Attention from others and to others	14. Altering one's state of consciousness, transcending the ordinary; Tranquility
5. Mirroring and echoing	15. Sexuality
6. Guidance; Idealism; Honor	16. Enjoyment or fun

7. Listening (others listen to and
    hear us)
	17. Freedom,
	        Independence

8. Being real	18. Nurturing

9. Participating
    Joining others,
    Taking part constructively,
    Sharing,
    Playing a part,
    Healthy family,
    Social contact
	19. Accomplishment
	    Mastery, "Power,"
	    "Control," Order,
	    Curiosity, Creativity
	    Having a sense of
	        completion
	    Making a contribution

10. Acceptance
    Freedom to be the Real You
    Tolerance of your feelings
    Validation
    Status
    Respect
    Belonging and love
    Others are aware of, take
    seriously and admire the Real You
	20. Unconditional love
	    (including connection with a Higher Power).
	
	Related to this & #14 above, Maslow added a *final need* to his hierarchy late in his career: *Transcendence*

Survival, Safety and Security — A newborn requires so much attention that someone must provide enough needs for its simple survival. At the barest minimum, this includes its safety and security for the first few years of its life. If that is not done, the child will have bothersome core issues and pain throughout its life. We gradually become able to assure these for ourself.

Safe Touching — From studies by Spitz, Montague, Pierce and others we know the importance of safe and healthy touching as a human need. Infants deprived of touching fail to thrive and grow, even if they get proper food, nourishment and protection. Touching is most powerful by appropriate skin to skin contact. Experiments with rabbits fed atherosclerosis-inducing diets show that those rabbits which are held and petted by the laboratory workers tend not to get atherosclerosis (hardening of the arteries). Those rabbits which are not held and petted tend to get atherosclerosis.

It seems that to feel connected and cared for, we need to be hugged and touched. Virginia Satir has suggested that we need several hugs a day as part of our health maintenance.

Attention — The child must be attended to—given attention. The mother or other parent figure(s) must attend the infant and child so that at least its safety, security and touching are met.

Mirroring and Echoing — The next need begins to validate the infant, child and even the adult, as a feeling and thinking being. Mirroring and echoing is when the mother reacts non-verbally by facial expression, posture, sounds and other movements so that the child realizes that it is understood.

At this point we understand that if the mother or other parent figure cannot provide these first few needs, the child's physical, mental-emotional and spiritual growth would likely be stunted. One reason may be that the mother herself is so impoverished and needy that she uses her infant to satisfy some of her own unmet needs. This is an amazing thing about infants. They can sense that mother is needy, and can eventually detect her specific needs and begin providing them for her. Of course, this carries a major price—the denial, stifling and stunting of the infant's own True Self. That price escalates as the child grows into an adult, with resulting physical, mental-emotional and spiritual pain and suffering.

Guidance — Guidance, also a part of helping the infant and child to develop and grow, may include advice, assistance, and any other form of help, verbal or non-verbal. It also includes modeling and teaching appropriate and healthy social skills.

Listening, Participating and Accepting — It is helpful to know that someone hears us, even if they do not always understand. Increasingly nourishing forms or types of listening are associated with numbers 8 through 20 on this Needs Hierarchy, including participation with the child in appropriate activities, and accepting the Real Self of the infant, child and eventual adult. The mother, other parent figure or concerned other is aware of, takes seriously and admires the child's Real Self. They demonstrate their acceptance by respecting, validating, and being tolerant of the feelings of the other's Real Self. This allows us the freedom to be our authentic self and to grow. Now, readers may see that some of their needs were not—perhaps are not—being met. Yet we are but half-way through this hierarchy of our human needs.

Opportunity To Grieve Losses and To Grow — With each hurt, loss or trauma that we experience, whether it be a real or a threatened loss, we have a need to grieve it—to work through the associated pain and suffering. To do so takes time. And when we grieve our losses to completion, we grow. I describe this process of grieving and growing in some detail in Chapters 15 and 16.

Support — Support implies that the friend or caretaker will not block the child's seeking, receiving input and creating, and will do everything possible to assure that their Real Self can fulfill its potential. Support includes actively doing whatever is possible to see that they can to grow and thrive.

Loyalty and Trust — Being supportive requires loyalty and trust from both the giver and the receiver. A person cannot betray another for long without causing serious damage to the relationship. In order to grow, the child and adult should feel trusted and be able to trust others (Chapter 17).

Accomplishment — On a basic level, achieving or accomplishing implies empowerment, "power," healthy "control," or the potential to master— and belief that the person can accomplish a task. On a higher level, this means not only completing the task, but also being aware that the task is satisfactorily complete. Perhaps the highest level of accomplishment is the feeling that one made a contribution, which offers meaning to the task.

Some people who grew up in troubled or dysfunctional families found it difficult to complete a task or a project or to make decisions. This is because they did not practice doing so with the guidance and support of an important other. By contrast, others from dysfunctional families may be high achievers in some areas, such as education or work, but are repeatedly unable to achieve in other areas, such as intimate relationships.

Altered Consciousness, Enjoyment and Fun — Classifying the alteration of one's state of consciousness as a human need is somewhat controversial. This is because of the folklore that altered consciousness implies using alcohol or other mood-changing drugs. Andrew Weil MD and others note that we have an innate —even a biological need— to periodically alter our conscious state, whether it be by daydreaming, laughing, playing sports, concentrating on a project or sleeping. Closely related to this is another need and also an altered state: enjoyment or having fun. Many children from troubled families have difficulty relaxing and having fun. Ability to be spontaneous and to play is a need and a characteristic of our Real Self.

Sexuality — Sexuality is often not mentioned as a human need. Rather than sexual intercourse alone, by sexuality I mean a range of potentials, from feeling good about being a man or a woman, to enjoying various aspects of being sexual, to discovering the man (animus) inside the psyche of the woman or the woman (anima) inside the man. Many of us who grew up in troubled homes may have difficulty with our sexual identity, functioning or enjoyment. Some of us may have been sexually abused, whether overtly or covertly.

Freedom — Having the freedom to risk, explore and do what is spontaneous and necessary is another human need. Along with this freedom comes responsibility. For example, spontaneity tends to be healthy, whereas impulsivity may work against our best interests.

Nurturing — The next-to-the-last highest order of human needs is nurturing; to provide any or all of the above needs to someone may be appropriate in some relationships. However, the nurturing person must be able to nurture and the person in need must be able to let go, to surrender, in order to be nurtured. In my observations of patients, their families, and of other people, this reciprocity is often uncommon in human interaction. It is not the child's job to nurture their parent, and when this happens repeatedly, it is a subtle form of child abuse or neglect.

Unconditional Love — This is our eventual need, and difficult to understand. I discuss it further in Chapters 12 and 21. Giving and receiving it is usually fulfilling. Attention to spirituality usually helps.

THE UNFULFILLED AND UNABLE PARENT

Rarely does anyone find a mother, other parent figure or close friend who is even capable of providing —or of helping us meet *all* of our needs—much less one who delivers them. In and outside of families there is usually no such person available. Thus, in our recovery, *we grieve* over not having had all our needs met as infants, children and even as adults. *Grieving* over the opposite—*getting* things that we didn't want or need—such as child mistreatment or abuse, is *also healing*.

Many mothers, fathers or other parent figures are themselves mentally and emotionally impoverished. A likely reason is that their needs were not met as infants, children and/or adults. They are thus so in need that they tend to use others in an unhealthy and inappropriate way to get *their* needs met. Alice Miller said that anyone in their immediate environment — anyone close to or near them, including infants and children— will be unconsciously used for their needs. In order to survive, the child who cannot develop a strong True Self compensates by developing an exaggerated false or co-dependent self.

At first it may seem inconceivable that a mother would use a vulnerable, helpless newborn infant to get her own needs met. Yet this occurs repeatedly in many troubled or dysfunctional families. In fact, getting pregnant and carrying a child to term in hope that someone (the as yet unborn child) will love *them* is sometimes primarily for the mother's *wants*, and not needs. Consider the difference between wants (what you don't really need) vs real needs (in Table).

GETTING FREE OF NEGLECTING MY NEEDS

Commonly found associated with the lower box contents in Figure 13.1 on page 148, neglecting our needs often leads to emotional pain and many problems, including relapses of PTSD, addictions and illness, as well as triggering core issues, relationship disruption and more emotional pain. By taking care of *getting our own needs met* and practicing *living in the upper section*, we can work through this common core issue time and again.

To be free and get what we want takes responsibility. Throughout this book I have woven the importance of taking responsibility for meeting our own needs (see the Index for other ways our needs are involved in this interesting process.)

FIGURE A.1. THE SPECTRUM OF COMPASSION

Feelings Response on Seeing Another Person Needy, Vulnerable or in Distress

Aggressive Detachment (ego, contempt)	Ordinary Detachment	Detached Attention (simple Observation)	Sympathy Feelings FOR/WITH	Empathy Feelings AS/IN	» Overarousal » Enmeshed » Projective Identification

e.g., in
Al-Anon,
ACA, CoDA

Healthy Boundaries

These feelings are learned and Inherent

...Modeled, Taught, *with* Limit setting

Some don't have these:

» Conduct disorder, e.g., Bullys

» ASPD

» Child Molesters

Each of these choices usually depends on the context in which we are involved with the other.

FIGURE A.2. RELATIONSHIP AMONG FOUR FORMS OF DEPENDENCE (REFERRED TO IN CHAPTER 18)

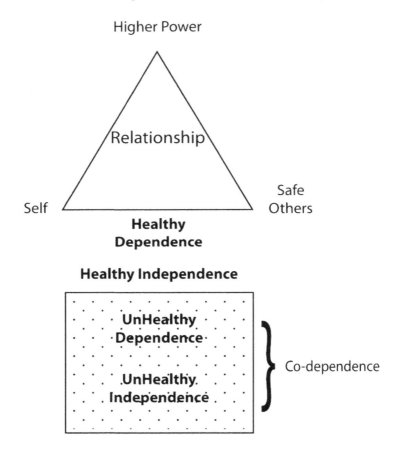

This figure shows the dynamic relationship of healthy and unhealthy dependence and independence, with the power of being in regular harmony with self, safe others and Higher Power as a way to recovery, healing and peace.

REFERENCES

1 Ames DR (2004) Inside the Mind Reader's Tool Kit: Projection and stereotyping in mental state inference. J Personality & Social Psych 87:3, 340--53

2 Amodeo J, Wentworth K (1986) *Being Intimate*: A Guide to Successful Relationships. Arkana/Penguin NY

3 Anonymous (1995) *Co-Dependence Anonymous.* (the CoDA Big Book) first edition, Co-Dependence Anonymous Inc, Phoenix AZ

3a Anonymous (2006) *Adult Children Alcoholic/Dysfunctional Families.* (the ACA Big Book) first edition, Torrance Ca

3b Anonymous (1995) *Alcoholics Anonymous.* (the AA Big Book) third edition, AA World Services, NYC, NY

4 Atkinson P (2011) on political correctness www.ourcivilisation.com/pc.htm
"Unless plain speaking is allowed, clear thinking is denied."

5 *As Bill Sees It*
www.inovadev.com/cafe/BigBook_PDF/AsBillSeesIt.pdf

6 Bach G, Goldberg H (1974) *Creative Aggression*: The art of assertive living. Garden City, NY: Doubleday

7 Beck M, (2012) *Finding Your Way In the Wild New World* Simon and Schuster, New York, NY.

8 Bloom S (1997). *Creating Sanctuary*: Toward the Evolution of Sane Societies. New York: Routledge

9 Breggin P (2007) *Brain Disabling Treatments in Psychiatry*: Drugs, Electroshock, and the Psychopharmaceutical Complex. Springer, NY

10 Brown B (2010) On numbing our vulnerability. bipolarblast.wordpress.com/2011/11/06/we-numb-vulnerability/

11 Brown B (2010) *The Gifts of Imperfection*: Let go of who you think you're supposed to be and embrace who you are. Hazelden, Center City, MN

12 Brown N, Amatea E (2000) *Love and Intimate Relationships:* Journeys of the Heart. Philadelphia, Bruner-Mazel

13 Brown NM, Amatea ES (2000) *Love and Intimate Relationships:* Journeys of the Heart. Brunner/Mazel Philadelphia, Penn.

14 Bryant FB Joseph V (2007) *Savoring: A New Model of Positive Experience.* Mahwah, New Jersey: Lawrence Erlbaum Associates.
(Bryant postulates four different skills needed to achieve savoring by controlling attention: a) avoiding negative rumination, b) confidence in avoiding negative outcomes, c) confidence in achieving positive outcomes, and d) confidence in savoring positive outcomes. He credits Silvan Tomkins's general images for paths of savoring. Mihály Csíkszentmihályi praises Bryant's work.)

15 Carver J (accessed 2 Dec 2011) www.mental-health-matters.com/anxiety/168-what-are-qbad-nervesq?start=1

16 Catherall DR (2007) *Emotional Safety*: viewing couples through the lens of affect. New York, Routledge

17 Campbell J (1949) *The Hero with a Thousand Faces*. Princeton University Press

18 Campbell J (2003) *The Hero's Journey:* Joseph Campbell on his life and work, 3rd edition, ed. Phil Cousineau. New World Library

19 Cermack TL, Brown S (1982) Interactional group therapy with the adult children of alcoholics. Intl J Group Psychotherapy 32:375-389

20 Cermack TL (1990) *Evaluating and Treating Adult-Children of Alcoholics.* Johnson Institute, Minneapolis

21 Cermack T (1986) *Diagnosing and Treating Co-Dependents.* Johnson Institute, Minneapolis

22 Cicchetti D, Ackerman BP, Izard CE (1995) Emotions and emotion regulation in developmental psychopathology [Special issue]. *Development and Psychopathology*, 7, 1-10

23 Cognitive Distortions: www.athealth.com/consumer/disorders/destructivethinking.html

24 Cognitive therapy: en.wikipedia.org/wiki/Cognitive_therapy

25 Conflicts www.internetmediator.com/medres/pg18.cfm

26 Csíkszentmihalyi M (1990), *Flow:* The Psychology of Optimal Experience, New York: Harper and Row

27 Dayringer R (1976) Fair Fight for Change: A therapeutic use of aggressiveness in couple counseling. J Marital & Family Ther. 2: 2, 115-30, April

28 Demos E. V. (1995). *Exploring affect:* The selected writings of Silvan Tomkins. Cambridge, England, New York, and Paris: Cambridge University Press.

29 Doverspike WF (2012) How Cognitive Distortions Cause Emotional Distress www.gapsychology.org/displaycommon.cfm?an=1& subarticlenbr=217

30 Ekman P (ed.) (2008). *Emotional Awareness*: Overcoming the Obstacles to Psychological Balance and Compassion: A Conversation Between the Dalai Lama and Paul Ekman. New York: Henry Holt and Company

31 Fairbairn WRD (1952) *Psychoanalytical Studies of the Personality*. Routledge, NY

32 Fischer B (1985) Workshop on shame. Baltimore MD

33 Fogarty TT (1973-83) Several papers, including the following: On Emptiness and Closeness Part 1 & 2; The Distancer and the Pursuer; Fusion; Triangles; Evolution of a Systems Thinker. In Compendium I, Center for Family Learning, New Rochelle, NY

34 Fossum MA, Mason MJ (1989) *Facing Shame*: Families in recovery. Norton, NY

35 Freyd JJ (1998) *Betrayal Trauma*: The logic of forgetting childhood abuse. Harvard University Press, Cambridge, Ma

36 Fun reference: Daniels BC (1995) *Puritans at Play*: Leisure and Recreation in Colonial New England. St Martin's Press, New York

37 Fun reference: www.comp.lancs.ac.uk/~dixa/papers/ECCE-fun-2004/ecce-alan-fun-panel.pdf

38 Friel JC, Friel LD (1990) Adult children: the secrets of dysfunctional families. Health Communications

40 Gravitz H, Bowden J (1987) *Recovery*: A Guide for Adult Children of Alcoholics. Touchstone, NY

41 Griffin J. (retrieved from www.clinical depression.co.uk/depression-article/ plus www.humangivens.com/joe-griffin/washington-times.html

42 Goleman D (1998) *Emotional Intelligence*. Bantam, NY

43 Goleman D (1998) *Working with Emotional Intelligence*. Bantam, NY

44 Guntrip H (1975) *Schizoid phenomena, object relations and the self*. International Universities Press, Madison, CT

45 Grieving www.hns.org/Portals/1/Stages%20of%20Grief.pdf from Center for Grief & Healing, Danvers, MA 01923, (978) 774-5100 www.griefandhealing.org

46 Griffin J, Tyrrell I (2003) *Human Givens*: A new approach to emotional health and clear thinking. HG Publishing, UK

47 Griffin J, Tyrrell I (2007) *How to Master Anxiety*: All you need to know to overcome stress, panic attacks, phobias, trauma, obsessions and more. HG Publishing, UK

48 Izard CE (1991) *The Psychology of Emotions*. New York: Plenum

49 Izard CE (1993) Four systems for emotion activation: Cognitive and non-cognitive processes. Psychological Review, 100, 68-90

50 Jackson GE: *Reconsidering Psychiatric Drugs*. Author House, Bloomington, IN 2005

51 Jackson GE: *Drug-Induced Dementia*: a perfect crime. Author House, Bloomington, IN 2009

52 James M, Savary L (1977) *A new self*: Self-therapy with transactional analysis. Reading, MA: Addison-Wesley

53 Johnson B (2005) *Emotional Health*: What emotions are and how they cause social and mental diseases. Trust Consent Publishing, Isle of White, UK

54 Katie B (2008) *Who Would You Be Without Your Story*? Hay House, NY

55 Kaufman G. (1985) *Shame: The Power of Caring* (2d ed.). Cambridge, MA: Schenkman Books

56 Klein M, Riviere J (1964) Love, guilt, and reparation in *Love, Hate, and Reparation.* Norton, NY, NY

57 Kohut H (1971) *The Analysis of the Self*. Intnl Univ Press, NY

58 Kurtz E, Ketcham K (1993) *The Spirituality of Imperfection*: Storytelling and the search for meaning. Bantam NY

59 Langer EJ (1975) *The Psychology of Control*. Sage, 1000 Oaks, Ca

60 L'Abate L (1977) Intimacy is sharing hurt feelings: A reply to David Mace. J Marital & Family Ther. 3:2, 13--16, April

61 Lewis M, Haviland-Jones JM, Feldman L (2010) *Handbook of Emotions*, 3rd Ed, Guilford Publications, NY

62 Lodge J (1972) Isn't life strange. Lyrics by author and sung by The Moody Blues. en.wikipedia.org/wiki/Isn%27t_Life_Strange *and*

www.youtube.com/watch?v=9WZZjXgJ4W8&feature
=results_main&playnext=1&list=PL2D0013FF6A366
A69

63 Malone TP, Malone PT (1987) *The Art of Intimacy*. Prentice Hall NY

64 Martin R (2002) *The Responsibility Virus*: How control freaks, shrinking violets (and the rest of us) can harness the power of true partnership. Basic Books, NY Chapter Section summarized in www.pearsoned.co.uk/bookshop/article.asp?item=5 73

65 Mason MJ (1986) *Intimacy*. Booklet, Hazelden, MN

66 Masterson JF (1988) *The Search for the Real Self*: Unmasking the personality disorders of our age. Collier Macmillan, NY

67 McCann E, Shannon D (1985) *The Two Step*: The Dance Toward Intimacy. Grove Press, NY

68 Miller A (1981) *Prisoners of Childhood*: The drama of the gifted child and the search for the true self. Basic Books New York, NY

69 Miller GA (1956) The magical number seven, plus or minus two: Some limits on our capacity for processing information. *Psychological Review*, 63:81–97

70 Moncrieff J: *The Myth of the Chemical Cure*: A Critique of Psychiatric Drug Treatment. Palgrave Macmillan, NY 2008

71 Murphy W, Whitfield CL, Whitfield B (2011) *Casey Anthony*: What Really Happened to Caylee and Why Truth Matters. Muse House Press, Atlanta, GA

72 Nathanson DL (1992) *Shame and Pride*: Affect, Sex, and the Birth of the Self. New York: W.W. Norton

73 Nathanson DL (ed.) (1987) *The Many Faces of Shame*. New York: Guilford

74 Obsessive love:
en.wikipedia.org/wiki/Obsessive_love

75 Osbon DK (1991) *Reflections on the Art of Living*: A Joseph Campbell companion. HarperCollins, NY

76 Peck MS (1998) *People of the Lie*: The hope for healing human evil. 2nd ed. Touchstone

77 Papp LM, Cummings EM, Goeke-Morey MC (2009) For richer, for poorer: Money as a topic of marital conflict in the home. *Family Relations, 58,* 91-103

78 Political correctness
en.wikipedia.org/wiki/Political_correctness

78a Rosen A (2010) *Lasting Transformation*: A guide to navigating life's journey. Balboa Press, Bloomington. IN

79 Sackett A, Meyvis T, Nelson L, Converse B, Sackett A (2010). You're having fun when time flies: the hedonic consequences of subjective time progression. *Psychological science* : a journal of the American Psychological Society / APS 21 (1): 111–117

80 Schema therapy website
www.schematherapy.com/id201.htm

80a Simonov PV (1986) *The Emotional Brain*: Physiology, Neuroanatomy, Psychology and Emotion. Springer, NY

80b Simos B (1979) *A Time to Grieve*: Loss As a Universal Human Experience. Families Intl, L.A. Ca

81 Solomon, Paul
www.paulsolomon.com/NewFiles/Paul%20Solomon%20Biography%20MSMG%201009.pdf

82 Stein W (1989) *On the Problem of Empathy*. In The Collected Works of Edith Stein, 3rd revised edition, ICS Publications, Washington DC

83 Teitelbaum SH (1999) *Illiusionment and Disillusionment*. Core issues in psychotherapy. Jason Aronson, Northvale NJ

84 Tomkins S (2008) *Affect Imagery Consciousness:* The Complete Edition. Two Volumes. New York: Springer

85 Tollefson W (2000) Incorporation therapy workshop, Tampa, FL

86 Weeks GR, L'Abate L (1982) *Paradoxical Psychotherapy*: Theory and Practice with Individuals, Couples, and Families. Brunner/Mazel New York, NY

87 Welwood J (2000) *Toward a Psychology of Awakening.* Shambhala Publications, Boston, MA

88 Whitaker R: *Anatomy of an Epidemic*: Magic Bullets, Psychiatric Drugs, and the Astonishing Rise of Mental Illness in America. Crown, NY 2010

89 Whitfield BH 2010 *The Natural Soul:* Unity with the Spiritual Energy that Connects Us. Muse House Press, Atlanta, GA

90 Whitfield CL (2010) Psychiatric drugs as agents of trauma. *Int J of Risk and Safety in Medicine* 22 (4)195-207

91 Whitfield CL (1987) *Healing the Child Within*: Discovery and recovery for adult children of dysfunctional families. Health Communications, Deerfield Beach, FL also *translated and published in* French, German, Spanish, Portuguese, Italian, Farsi, Japanese, Croatian and Korean translation editions

92 Whitfield CL (1990) *A Gift to Myself*: A personal workbook and guide to Healing the Child Within. Health Communications, Deerfield Beach, FL also *translated and published in* a French edition

93 Whitfield CL (1991) *Co-dependence* - Healing the Human Condition. The new paradigm for helping professionals and people in recovery. Health Communications, Deerfield Beach, FL 1991

94 Whitfield CL (1993) *Boundaries and Relationships*: Knowing, Protecting and Enjoying the Self. Health Communications, Deerfield Beach, FL - also *translated and published in* French and Spanish editions

95 Whitfield CL (1995) *Memory and Abuse*: Remembering and Healing the Effects of Trauma. Health Communications, Deerfield Beach, FL

96 Whitfield CL, Silberg J, Fink P (eds.) (2002) *Misinformation Concerning Child Sexual Abuse and Adult Survivors*. Haworth Press NY

97 Whitfield CL (2003) *The Truth about Depression*: Choices for Healing. Health Communications, Deerfield Beach, FL, (800-851-9100) (translated into Portuguese) Two chapters published in Goldberg R (2006) *Taking Sides*: Clashing Views in Drugs & Society (7th Ed) McGraw-Hill, Dubuque, IA)]

98 Whitfield CL: *The Truth about Mental Illness*: Choices for Healing. Health Communications, Deerfield Beach, FL, 2004

99 Whitfield CL (2003) *My Recovery: A Personal Plan for Healing.* Health Communications, Deerfield Beach, FL

100 Whitfield CL, Whitfield BH, Prevatt J, Park R (2006) *The Power of Humility*: Choosing Peace over Conflict in Relationships. Health Communications, Deerfield Beach, FL

101 Whitfield CL (2010) *Choosing God:* A Bird's Eye View of A Course in Miracles. Muse House Press, Atlanta, GA

102 Whitfield CL (2010) *Teachers of God*: Further Reflections on A Course in Miracles. Muse House Press, Atlanta, GA

103 Whitfield CL (2011) *Not Crazy:* You May Not Be Mentally Ill - Misdiagnosed and mistreated with drugs that don't work well or make you worse. Important information withheld from you by the Drug Industry, Psychiatry, Government, and others. Muse House Press, Atlanta, GA

104 Whitfield CL (1984) *Alcoholism, Other Drug Problems & Spirituality*: Stress Management and Serenity During Recovery. Perrin & Tregett, Rutherford, NJ

105 Whitfield CL (2006) The Doctor's Opinion. in *Adult Children: Alcoholic/Dysfunctional Families*. [the first "Big Book" of Adult Children of Alcoholics] Torrance, Ca/Brainerd, MN

106 Whitfield CL, Whitfield BH (in process for 2013) *Engaging the Muse*: Using Creativity in Everyday Life. Muse House Press, Atlanta, GA

INDEX

MORE BOOKS BY MUSE HOUSE PRESS AUTHORS

OTHER HELPFUL BOOKS BY *THE WHITFIELDS*

Dr. Whitfield explains in some detail how the reader can use practical and proven non-drug techniques and recovery aids. Caution: This book contains an indictment of the psychiatric drug industry and an enlightening exposure of their dogma for the people who are taking these brain disabling drugs and those who care for them.

—Peter R. Breggin, MD, Psychiatrist and author of *Medication Madness*

This is not an easy book to read. It contains real-life pain, sadness and loss. Some of us have suffered like Carole did --and worse-- yet in reading this book – we discover healing. There is help here. And most importantly, there is hope within these pages for anyone who has been severely and re-peatedly traumatized, abused and/or neglected in childhood. Whitfield quotes from Carole's documentary: "The thunder-storms are just as beautiful as a sunny day. And so is life!"

—Donald Brennan from the Foreword

OTHER HELPFUL BOOKS BY CHARLES L. WHITFIELD, M.D.

Humility involves relationships. These include our relationships with our self, others, and if we choose, the God of our understanding. We can begin to define humility as having openness to learning more about these three relationships. And it is more. In The Power of Humility, the authors explore humility – and how we can use it to our benefit – from the perspective of all three of these relationships.

The authors of this breakthrough book, the power of humility is that it is the key to better relationships – with self, others and God – and inner peace.

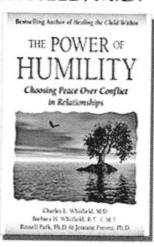

Best-selling author Charles Whitfield, M.D., offers clarity, skills and structure to help you take charge of your recovery by creating a personalized and workable program. Instead of merely treating the symptoms of your problem, Dr. Whitfield shows you how to uncover its physical, mental and spiritual roots, and use your own personal power as your most valuable healing tool. You'll learn how to overcome any issues that are inhibiting your healing, including resolving past traumas and connecting to a spiritual source.

Lightning Source UK Ltd.
Milton Keynes UK
UKOW04f1157091117
312433UK00002B/407/P

9 781935 827108